ROARING RESILIENCE
FINDING GRIT IN THE LION'S DEN

ADRIENNE N. SPIRES

Copyright © 2024 by Adrienne N. Spires
All rights reserved.

No part of this publication may be reproduced, stored in a retrieval system, or transmitted in any form or by any means, electronic, mechanical, photocopying, recording, scanning, or otherwise, without the prior written permission of the author.

ROARING RESILIENCE
Finding Grit in the Lion's Den

Adrienne N. Spires
adriennespires7@gmail.com

ISBN 978-1-943342-39-6

Printed in the United States of America
Destined To Publish
www.destinedtopublish.com

DEDICATION

My memoir is for women who started in a love nest and then found themselves prey in a lion's den. They thought it would be a challenge to live free. This book is about finding hope, encouragement, and faith in the grips of domestic violence.

ACKNOWLEDGMENTS

First and foremost, I give thanks and praise to God for blessing me throughout this tedious writing process and allowing me to complete my book successfully.

I want to express extreme gratitude to my family and friends, especially my parents, whose wisdom and grit will forever guide me. A special shout-out to my husband, Yarann, aka James, who said, "Your book will be your new business card." To my sister, Dee Dee, who encouraged me to tell my story and was going to be my ghostwriter but ghosted me. However, in exchange, she became the unpaid editor. To my children and grandchildren, who make me "level up" in every aspect and are the center of my joy. To Shnell, who praise danced my authorship from Illinois to Cali.

To the friends who posed that question over the years, "How long have you been writing your book?" you know exactly who you are! To my colleague and friend Shandra, who became my sister-friend; I refused to ask her to review the manuscript because I was afraid of re-traumatization from her blood-red ink pen when she reviewed my research papers from graduate school.

Acknowledgments

Writing a book about my life was a huge undertaking and an ambivalent walk down memory lane. I'm forever appreciative of my literary coach, Deborah Anthony, for her expertise, ongoing encouragement, and black girl to black girl pep talks: "Let's get this book done (smirk, smile, roaring laughter)." In addition, Marilyn Alexander, the CEO of Destined to Publish, was my high school classmate and a journalist for the school's newspaper. Destiny brought us together 32 years after graduation so the journalist turned publisher could bring my story to life.

Finally, to all those who poured endlessly into me: my mentors Gayle Jeffries, Janice Mitchell, and Aunt Janie Johnson, rest in peace!

FOREWORD

When I found out our mother was pregnant, I was excited because I wanted a little brother. Then Adrienne arrived. Not a boy. Even when she wasn't crying, she had inherited the Young family's glassy eyes, so she looked like she was about to cry. To my four-year-old ears, it seemed like she cried all the time. Little did I know that this was the beginning of her learning to advocate for herself.

Readers will be introduced to her origin story and understand how insidious domestic violence and abuse occur within families. She provides a view into how love can turn dangerous and the longer-term impact on survivors and their children.

Over the years, I've watched her grit as a mother, wife, sister, daughter, friend, and advocate. Adrienne has always been resilient and has overcome many obstacles. So, when she said she wanted to write a book to help others, I did not doubt that she would deliver an inspiring story.

Foreword

It is incredibly brave of her to share her journey as a survivor and non-offending parent so that others know how to face challenges head-on with faith, not fear. Our parents would be proud of you, Adrienne, for turning your trauma into a testimony.

I'm also proud that that little crying baby is my sister ... who Roars in the Lion's Den!

Janie D. Young-Davis

TABLE OF CONTENTS

Chapter I: Ain't No Party Like a South Side Party 1
    Politics According to "Black Folks". 1
    Family Get-Together 3
    The Way We Praise the Almighty. 5
    The Beauty of Chi-Town 8
    Whose House? Young's House 10

Chapter II: Funkin' for Jamaica 14
    The Summer Sizzle of '83 14
    The Fresh Years @ the V 17
    Prom of '85 23
    Fast Times @ Ford City Shopping Mall. 24

Chapter III: Invincible Love 27
    Sr. Year Class of '87. 27
    Stork Introduction (1988). 31
    Reaching for Higher Ed 37
    Stork Visit (1991) 39

Table of Contents

Chapter IV: New Beginnings: Chambana 43
    Mama Dreamt of Fish 47

Chapter V: Honeymoon Phase. 48
    Third Stork Visit Was a Charm, 1992? 48
    Inaugural Marriage Conference & Nuptial. 52

Chapter VI: Wet Behind the Ears
(Tension-Building Phase). 55
    Say No to Drugs, I Wish!. .56
    Hello 911 58
    The Stork Returns with Two Gifts, '95 63

Chapter VII: Explosion Phase: Black, Blue, and Broken . . .67
    Acute Victim 73
    Guilt and Shame. 77

Chapter VIII: "A Man Has Always Wanted to Lay
Me Down But He Never Wanted to Pick Me Up"
– Eartha Kitt. 78
    "But He Never Wanted to Pick Me Up". 85

Chapter IX: The Unbearable Escalation. 88
    Separate to Live 88
    Exhale. 94
    Happily Divorced 97
    Rebuilt & Repositioned Family:
    Dublin Street Church of Christ 98

Table of Contents

Chapter X: Turned My Tassel 103
    Graduate Studies 103
    The Shock. 106

Chapter XI: Inducted Into the Non-Offending
Parent Club. 109
    The Trauma. 109
    Telling the Whole Truth, So Help Me God 115
    Means of Escape, Sensual Distraction 120

Chapter XII: The Psychological Process 129
    Individual Counseling. 129
    Faith & Spiritual Guidance 130

Chapter XIII: "It's Easier to Build Strong Children
Than to Repair Broken Men"- Fredrick Douglass. 134
    Introducing Teen Mothers to Their Own
    Expertise, 2006-2009 134
    Advocacy for the Survival of Survivors 141
    Writing Sample 152

Chapter XIV: "Blessed Shalt Thou Be in the City,
and Blessed Shalt Thou Be in the Field"
(Deuteronomy 28:3-5, KJV) 156
    The Apology. 160
    Colleague-Friends in the Pasadena Office 167

Table of Contents

Chapter XV: Project Fate 175
    Statements of Gratitude 182
    Epilogue 188
    Dear Reader 189

Notes 191

"He who is not angry when there is just cause for anger is immoral. Why? Because anger looks to the good of justice. And if you can live amid injustice without anger, you are immoral as well as unjust."

~ Thomas Aquinas

CHAPTER 1

AIN'T NO PARTY LIKE A SOUTH SIDE PARTY

Politics According to "Black Folks"

Some of my fondest childhood memories growing up on the South Side of Chicago are of the Friday night family get-togethers at 1619 West Garfield Avenue. My immediate family of nine, my mom, dad, five sisters—Jan, Cheryl, Genia, Janie aka Dee Dee, Sylvia aka Nicky—and one brother, Lil Gene, enjoyed attending the festivities. My grandmother and aunt owned a three-flat apartment building where three generations lived. Friday nights were a cross between a Mississippi juke joint and a black barbershop—also known as the black man's country club—and a political roundtable, or better yet, a think tank. My daddy and his five brothers, Walter Jr. Mane, Thomas Buddy Boy, Edward Ed, Frank, and Charles, were profound thinkers because their father had groomed them to be so. They had to be thinkers to be able to thrive as black men during the Jazz Age, the Great Depression, World War II, the Golden Age of Capitalism, the Civil Rights Movement, the Third Great Awakening, Reaganomics, and a decade of greed. To withstand those times, they had to have impeccable grit. Black men had to be courageous and persistent to navigate historical racism, oppression, and lynching to participate in the American Dream. According to the U.S. Constitution, kidnapped, tortured, and enslaved Africans/Black Americans are three-fifths of a person. I applaud the three-fifths, whose free labor built America into a world superpower and who have always shown up 100% for every war America initiated, allied, and executed.

My father's five brothers served in the U.S. Army during the Korean War and WWII. The reasons for these wars were to liberate South Korea from the north and to eradicate the rise of militarism in Germany and Japan, respectively. Ironically, when my uncles and other black U.S. soldiers returned to the South Side of Chicago, they were not able to receive services from the U.S. Veteran Hospital because the hospital was located in a segregated community where black people were not allowed. So, my uncles and other black soldiers had to go to St. Louis, Missouri, to receive the exact medical services that were denied them in Chicago.[1]

My grandfather Walter Young Sr. and his brother Samuel L. Young Sr. had to flee Natchez, Mississippi, because a white man told them they were "too big for their britches." That metaphoric statement meant they needed to leave ASAP to avoid being hung by their britches. Also, Natchez was known for being one of the most active slave trading cities in Mississippi.[2] In 1919, my grandfather and uncle journeyed north to Chicago. Unbeknownst to them, the Chicago Race Riot of 1919 was brewing. A total of 23 blacks were killed, and 15 whites were too, "after white Americans started a racial conflict against black Americans"[3] The racial tension spilled over into many institutions and systems, such as education, the labor market, and housing. This propelled my grandfather and great-uncle to strategize to help start the first black Painter Local Labor Union #1332. In recognition, Painter Local 1332 celebrated its centennial anniversary on August 20, 2020.[4] These were some of the historical conversations discussed at Friday night gatherings.

Family Get-Together

When I entered the building, I could smell the aroma of frying chicken wings and fish, and the walls were bumping with the sounds of rhythm and blues, including Sam Cooke tunes. From 1976 to 2019, My cousin Mike, aka Big Mike, was the designated family DJ. When my family and I reached the first-floor apartment, the door would fling open, accompanied by a "Hey, y'all." The boisterous greeting would erase those ridiculous thoughts if you weren't sure if you were welcome to the festivities. Some family and friends would be watching TV in the living room and engaging in conversations. Now, the place to be was the dining room down the hall, where bid whist, dirty hearts, and spades card games took place. The sound of playing cards slamming onto the card table could be heard. And yes, you could hear it, followed by "NEXT!" meaning the losing team must relinquish their seats for the new team, who imagined themselves shouting the winning roar: "Next!"

When I finally reached the kitchen, I was able to see the crispy chicken wings and fried fish (in two separate frying pans, of course), spaghetti with hamburger meat, potato salad, sweet potato pies, and a big bottle of Louisiana hot sauce. The matriarch, Lubertha Young, also known as Mama, and Aunt Annie, the oldest sister of the eight children, were the soulful chefs. The interactions in the kitchen resembled scenes from a soul food cooking show, with a side of laughter from the soul, and the talk show *The View*, except with an all-black cast. This cast of melanated women talked about everything from press and curls to sewing patterns and the famous church hats.

My grandmother (Mama) and Aunt Sister, the younger daughter, looked distinguished in their church hats. They could've walked down the Ebony Fashion Fair runway. Black women possess a particular presence when wearing church hats. Actually, they possess a presence, period.

So, my grandmother (Mama) and Aunt Sister—her birth name is Luberta after her mom, but the family affectionately called her Sister—of course, they wore those hats at church. They belonged to Mount Moriah Missionary Baptist Church on the South Side of Chicago. Our family were members for at least five generations. I distinctly remember Aunt Sister and her choir members hosting a tea at Mount Moriah, and this is when my family and I had an opportunity to dress up and wear some beautiful dresses and cute little hats. I wore a long pink dress and a pair of white patent leather shoes and had the cutest press and curl hair style. The tea took place in the basement of the church. All the tables had white tablecloths, decorative centerpieces, cloth napkins, and flatware. The menu consisted of soul food delicacies such as homemade coconut cakes, sweet potato pies, and red punch. The decorations had a southern and classy feel to them and made me think about the rich lineage I was a part of. I thank God for the early introduction to church and spirituality. I'm adamant these experiences contributed to my spiritual journey and the person I am today.

The Way We Praise the Almighty

Also, when I reminisce about my early days in the church, I think about listening to the popular radio stations that highlight gospel music throughout the week. Every Sunday, Jacquie Haselrig was the DJ on WGCI 107.5 FM gospel hour. She took everyone to church figuratively and literally with songs by the Canton Spiritual, Shirley Caesar, Rev. Timothy Wright, Walter Hawkins, Albertina Walker, and Florida Mass Choir. Some of my favorite songs were "My Liberty" by Southeast Inspirational Choir featuring Yolanda Adams before she became a solo artist, "Jesus Can Work It Out" by the Cosmopolitan Church of Prayer Choir featuring Diane Williams, and Sam Cooke's "Touch the Hem of His Garment." You could hear people blasting WGCI from their homes and from cars driving down the street.

Every weekday morning, I woke up to Purvis Spann the Blues Man Morning Show on WVON AM. Purvis Spann was known as the stepfather of soul and was influential in the development of the Chicago blues music scene. He was one of the first DJs for Chicago's famous Chess Records. Each morning, he opened with Marvin Gaye's rendition of "His Eye Is On The Sparrow" while my dad cooked a hearty breakfast before he went to work—usually cheesy eggs, grits with sugar (yes, I said sugar), Jimmy Dean sausages and biscuits, and orange juice.

WVON closed their daily program with "Open Our Eyes" by the Gospel Clefs before the Carl Rowan Report. I found that song particularly interesting because that was the last song played every night before bedtime. I often wondered if the real intent of that chosen song was for all listeners to inject "God, open our eyes" into their nightly prayers.

Listening to these political commentators and my father made me hypervigilant about the political world, especially in Chicago, where I was 10 years old. My dad told me politics is infused in every system and institution, and no one could tell me otherwise. For example, school districts' budgets are determined by property taxes paid in the community. Unfortunately, black communities were always undervalued and still are to this day. One of my all-time favorites is to beware of feasibility studies and study sessions. My dad said they have been a stalling tactic since slavery.

I grew more interested in the Chicago machine as well as in blue and red states. Politics influences every fiber of our life from education to religion. In 1966, black churches in Chicago were swayed by the "machine" not to welcome Martin Luther King Jr. into their pulpit to speak about the discriminatory rental and mortgage lending practices impacting black folks. I'm sure members of those churches were impacted by the very reasons MLK came to Chicago to advocate. Rev. Clay Evans, the founder and senior pastor of Fellowship Missionary Baptist Church, was the only black pastor who let Martin Luther King Jr. speak in his pulpit.⁵ The "machine" was so powerful that faith leaders overlooked members who paid tithes and offerings; served on the usher board, deacon board, youth ministries, and mother's board; gave to the building fund; and experienced the disparaging housing conditions. In addition to the machine, Chicago is also known for the various communities within the city, like Englewood.

I had a pretty typical upbringing in Englewood on the South Side of Chicago. Kids who lived on the block regularly walked to school together. We laughed, we raced, and sometimes we ate some candy on our way to school. It was just a good environment where we had fun, and there was no bullshit. We didn't have to worry about anyone snatching us. Don't get me wrong, there were some fights, but we were a strong, tight-knit community. Missing children's faces didn't start appearing on the back of milk cartons until the late 1980s, so we had a chance to enjoy our childhood without the trauma of kidnapping.

Recently, I heard a story about something that took place in the late 1970s. There were some gang members trying to recruit the young black boys on our block and the next block over. As I stated before, our community was close-knit. The black fathers in the community, including my father, Mr. Jones, Mr. Green, Mr. Johnson, Mr. Dye, and some other dads, protected their sons. They met some of the gang members with baseball bats, and rumor is maybe some revolvers, to make sure they got their point across and assured the gang members that their sons were not recruitable. What a fascinating story. Imagine if more communities had more men who protected their homes, protected their children, and made sure that their community was protected from potential gang activities.

The Beauty of Chi-Town

Another love of Chicagoans was playing softball. We would play softball on a street corner or even in the alley. That's how much we loved softball on the South Side of Chicago. We played softball against other communities or even against other neighborhood blocks. Now, mind you, this was not an organized softball team. There were some organized softball teams in the park district, but we would just have these games in our community. We played softball games before school started. The gym teacher, the librarian, an administrator, and a fifth-grade teacher were part of our softball teams. I must admit, I was a really good softball player. I could knock the shit out of a softball.

One summer, I hit a home run and busted my neighbor's window. I was excited our team won, but I wasn't particularly happy when I had to use my allowance to pay for the broken window. The position I liked best was shortstop because I could catch a flying ball and a fast ball.

Softball and baseball are such a phenomenon in Chicago that there are two baseball teams: the Chicago Cubs on the North Side and the White Sox on the South Side. My family and I rooted for the best Chicago team, the White Sox. We used to go to numerous White Sox baseball games at Comiskey Park. We went on hat, bat, rain jacket, and patch day. My ultimate goal was to catch an actual baseball. So, one year, my eighth-grade teacher, Ms. Steveson, took some students to a night game. We arrived early while the team was practicing before the game. One of the players hit the ball into the stand about a foot away from me. I counted my eggs before they hatched. I was laughing, saying I got it like I just hit the lottery. Low and behold, the concession guy carrying drinks made his way to the ball before I could grab it. I thought, what the F...! My teacher and classmates were like, "You're working; give her the ball." He had the audacity to say, "You snooze, you lose." I blessed (cursed) him out as loud as I could cognitively! What was so funny about that story was that I saw Bernie Mac in an interview about 15 years later sharing how he used to work at White Sox Park. I was pondering if he was the one who swiped my baseball from me. He fit the description. I didn't realize how much I really wanted that ball until I tried to put Bernie Mac at the scene.

One thing I didn't snooze on was being a part of the fun Chicago had to offer, especially the "illest" (= to be among the best of something but in a unique groundbreaking manner; to raise the bar; to change the game; to surpass) community on the South Side, which is Englewood. I refer to it as the real Englewood, not Inglewood, California.

I must admit Englewood helped raise me because the community in the 1970s and '80s was like a suburb, except it had charisma. It was clean and had small businesses like candy stores, restaurants, dry cleaners, Harold's Chicken, auto mechanic shops, shoe shops, and record stores. We also had black-owned beauty supply stores. I imagine it took much longer for the black dollars to leave Englewood.

Even with the humid summers, Chicago was like a big block party coupled with black liberation and a touch of black history. People hosted house parties in the basement of their homes, which were quite popular and included juking to house music. For example, the Jungle Brothers' "I'll House You" and "Let No

Man Put Asunder" by First Choice were really big songs, as well as slow dancing to Luther Vandross' "A House Is Not a Home." My friend Veronica and I hosted our first house party in the summer of 1982. We were only 12 and 13 years old. We passed out pluggers within a two-mile radius. A plugger was an invite on an index card with all the party details: when, where, who the hosts are, and the cost with and without the plugger. Guests with pluggers paid $1.50, and it was $2 without. Veronica and I split about $100, which was pretty good for our first house party. Veronica's father, Julius, was the DJ, and his favorite song was "Gypsy Woman" by The Impressions, released in 1963. We had some albums of our own to play, and my cousins Karen and Lucy were bringing some of my cousin Mike's records to spin at the party. It was one and a half hours into the party, and there was no sign of Karen, Lucy, or the records. Julius waved me and Veronica over to the DJ table to tell us, "I'm down to the last album, and Gypsy is next on the playlist." We looked at each other and screamed, "NO!" Our cool neighbor, Greg, came to our rescue with house music, cool pop, and slow jam albums. People came from all over the South Side, and a few from the West Side, to take part in the house party. Veronica and I were the youngest at our very first house party.

Whose House? Young's House

We lived in a multi-level house. My dad ran a regimented house. We only had one bathroom, so we had to shuffle in and shuffle out quickly. My parents expected us to wash and iron our clothes over the weekend for the upcoming school week. My father didn't want us to do laundry during the week because "it would cause the electric and water bill to go up." My dad was quite frugal and quite savvy when it came to budgeting. He made sure everything was paid on time and in order. To control the bills, he was very adamant that we couldn't touch the thermostat in his house. To deal with Midwest weather, we dressed light and took showers to stay cool per my dad in the summer and wore house shoes and heavy pajamas during the winter.

Also, my dad didn't want the house to look like seven children lived there, so starting at the age of four, my Saturdays were spent waking up at 5 a.m. to eat breakfast and clean. We ate the heartiest breakfast on Saturday and Sunday mornings, consisting of grits with sugar (not salt), cheesy scrambled eggs, Jimmy Dean's breakfast sausages, biscuits, and Daddy's freshly squeezed orange juice. I thoroughly enjoyed the smothered beef liver with onions and gravy and rice or smothered pork chops and potatoes.

My siblings and I had to wash walls and baseboards in the house with our own buckets and sea sponges. I posed a question very loudly: "Who the hell will come to people's houses and inspect their baseboards?" No one responded because I said it in my mind. I knew it was best not to verbalize it unless I wanted to incur consequences and repercussions. On the other hand, I didn't really mind because we were working to the sounds of Sam Cooke's "Everybody Loves to Cha Cha Cha" and Simon & Garfunkel's "Slip Slidin' Away" playing on the hi-fi record player. Sometimes we had dance breaks in between cleaning, such as when my dad would do his famous dance, "the washing machine." He thought he was getting down. Honestly, I never heard anyone ever mention or do that dance until 1997, about 20 years later, in the movie *Selena*. Selena's father asked her mother to teach

Selena the dance steps while they were at the beach. The actual name is Cumbia, and the dance tends to move in a circular or spiraling shape. It originated in the country Colombia during the war for independence from Spain. My dad's moves were the direct opposite of Cumbia, more like an aerobic exercise twisting his upper body. I know the description sounds awkward—so were his moves.

Usually, we completed chores by 8:30-9 a.m. Sometimes, if we didn't have planned activities, we watched *American Bandstand* hosted by Dick Clark and *Soul Train* hosted by Don Cornelius. One of my favorite memories of *Soul Train* was when Joe Tex performed his song "Ain't Gonna Bump No More (With No Big Fat Woman)." He was doing the dance "the bump" on stage with a voluptuous black woman toward the end of his performance. I was only eight years old at the time, and it was the cutest performance I had ever seen.

Most importantly, I was perfectly fine with the morning routine because I always looked forward to the spoils in the form of an allowance every other Saturday.

In addition to a clean and tidy house, there were fun times. We had a lot of fun in the front of the basement, which was the family and games room. The left side had a round dining room table and chairs and a wooden case with board games. There was also an air hockey and a ping-pong table. The other side had a rust-colored sectional couch and cocktail table and a wooden TV stand. Numerous holiday gatherings, card games, and birthday parties were hosted at the house, especially in the basement. My family had many traditions. I remember my baby sister, Nicky, and my birthday parties would turn into an adult Tonk card game and a jam session with hits. At a lot of the parties, cousin Mike became the "volunteered" DJ and/or graced us with karaoke. My parents were a team, which made all nine of us a solid unit.

For most of my youth, I was my father's copilot. Sometimes, Nicky and I would go to work with him on Saturdays. He was a union painter for the City of Chicago Housing Authority (CHA) for 30 years. He also had his own painting business on the side. Nicky and I would wash the walls and tape the baseboards before he started to paint. Obviously, people pay attention to their baseboards. Daddy, the foreman, provided breakfast and lunch along with a handsome salary.

Some of the best outings with my dad and Nicky were our visits to the flea market and Maxwell Street Market, which was offensively called Jew Town. My dad would let us buy loads of toys and other items. One of my funniest memories is of when Nicky and I were hurrying toward a crowd gathered in front of a vendor's table. My dad told us, "Never run toward a crowd; go in the opposite direction to avoid trouble." But we all walked to the table only to find a man trying to sell an empty fishbowl. He claimed the fish were magical and would reappear very soon. My dad and another gentleman laughed so hard. Then the man asked the vendor if he thought the "fish got lost in Lake Michigan." The crowd burst out in laughter. Then my dad said, "Let's go, and never buy anything that magical."

CHAPTER 11

FUNKIN' FOR JAMAICA
by: Tom Browne

The Summer Sizzle of '83

In the summer of '83, it was sizzling! I had just graduated from eighth grade from John P. Altgeld Elementary School. One day, I caught a glimpse of this cute guy across the street sitting on my neighbor Miranda's front porch. He saw me with my friends Lisa M., Lisa W., and Veronica, along with my sisters Cheryl and Nicky, hanging out on the front porch. He made his way from across the street to introduce himself.

"Hi, my name is Eddie."

We all exchanged the same pleasantries: "Hi, my name is Eddie." We were such smart asses. I played it cool. I gave him no eye contact, like he wasn't handsome. Eddie took it upon himself to tell us he would grace us with his presence for the entire summer. He was going to babysit for his aunt Miranda to make some extra money for his senior year in high school. Also, he told us he was on his high school football team and practice would be held approximately a mile away at Ogden Park.

I asked Eddie, "What position do you play?"

He said, "Noseguard."

I then posed another question: "Do you ride the bench, or are you fast on your feet?"

Eddie said with a sly grin, "No, I don't ride the bench."

Eddie was my "bee eye sweetie" (a term my grandmother, Mama Sarah, used to describe a guy you were smitten with and dating). He was about 5'7" and a sleek 150 pounds, with a non-greasy, carefree curl faded on the sides, a caramel complexion, medium-brown eyes, and thick and precisely shaped eyebrows as if they were threaded, which added to his appeal. He resembled a younger version of Gregory Abbott, the R&B singer who sang "Shake You Down," released in 1986. Both of us were able to relate to the alluring lyrics.

In addition to Eddie's attractive appearance, he was quite astute in math and science. His goal was to become a nurse or doctor or something in the medical field. I'm going to be honest, I wasn't really that interested in his academic aspirations at the time. However, his senior year in high school he majored in nursing and graduated with high marks. We built a really good relationship, with dates at Ford City Shopping Mall and eating at Burger King and Nancy's Pizza. We talked about sports and laughed with each other. Most of our time and fun took place on the block. My friends and I would play touch football with Eddie and sometimes hang out at the park. One time we raced from the beginning of the block to the end. Surprisingly, I won and asked him, "Are you sure you don't ride the bench?" We both looked at each other at the same time and fell out laughing.

Then, he said, "Your dimples make your smile unique." My response was that I'm pretty unique.

"How so?" Eddie asked.

"I was born the day the man landed on the moon: July 20, 1969."

Another exceptional story per my mama: She was in labor with me. At the same time, she was on the phone listening to some juicy gossip, and she figured she had plenty of time to get to the hospital because this was her seventh pregnancy. According to Mom, she was a pro by this time. The paddy wagon (a police van to transport criminals) was dispatched instead of an ambulance to transport her to the hospital. While my mother was being transported to the county hospital, I was born in the back of the paddy wagon. It was bad enough that I entered the world like a criminal, but then someone thought it was cute to give me the nickname Paddy. Sweet Jesus!

Well, I must confess I was a little mischievous—a very little. So, Eddie gave me my first hickeys. I had hickeys on my neck and wore a couple of T-shirts with collars or something to hide them from my mom, but this one particular time he gave me a hickey on each dimple. I really have cute dimples. Afterwards, I was sitting at the dining room table talking with my sisters Cheryl and Genia. Then, our mom came and sat at the table with us. I totally forgot that I had two hickeys on my dimples. I had tried to stay out of my mother's sight for a couple of days. My mom said, "Paddy, what's wrong with your face? Are you breaking out?"

And I said, "I think I am; I have had these things on my face, and I don't know what's causing it."

Cheryl looked up at me and bugged her eyes like she couldn't believe I just told a bald-faced lie to our mother. I knew exactly how I got the hickeys posing as blemishes. About 15 years in the future, I told my mother about the little white lie about the blemishes. I was laughing while sharing the juvenile memory. She was like, "Ha ha, hell." Then we both laughed out loud.

One night, Eddie and I were sitting on Miranda's porch, and Eddie asked me to be his prom date. Carefully, I said, "Sure." The prom was nine months away, in May 1984.

Sadly, the summer was coming to an end. The night before Eddie went home, we all hung out on the block and danced to Michael Jackson's *Thriller* album. Eddie couldn't get into the songs, no matter how many times I played it. We closed the party out with Tom Browne's "Funkin' for Jamaica." The next afternoon we said our sweet goodbyes and promised to continue to date throughout the school year. That was one fantastic summer!

The Fresh Years @ the V

The fall of 1983 was my freshman year at Chicago Vocational High School, aka CVS or the V. CVS was one of the largest high schools in the city of Chicago. My freshman class consisted of about 1,100 students. The first day of school, I had a chance to reintroduce myself to some of my classmates that I met during freshmen orientation. My friend Veronica from the block accompanied me to a few CVS football games, and we met up with some of my classmates. I never had a chance to attend the limited football games Eddie played. He had to quit the team because his nursing program was quite rigid. Eddie and I were able to spend two weekends together before we broke up in November 1983. I don't recall what the spat was about that caused us to part. He told my sister Cheryl he was upset that I didn't look back when I left his aunt's house. So that was that. My sizzle had fizzled.

According to my class schedule, I was enrolled in a sewing class for the whole school year. If my memory serves me correctly, I didn't sign up for sewing. I attended class for about one week and pleaded to be transferred to the auto mechanic class. Looking back, I wish I had stayed in the sewing course, because my maternal grandmother, Mama Sarah, and paternal aunt Annie were great seamstresses. Also, Mama Sarah was a milliner. She made and sold the nicest hats. As I reflect, I realize I missed the opportunity to master a valuable craft with the help of my family.

My new schedule for the school year was auto mechanics, graphic arts, electronics, and welding. I was the only girl in class until another girl joined later in the semester. Classes were enlightening and fun. During the last quarter of the semester, I was ready for welding. This class was taking place after the popular movie *Flashdance* with Jennifer Beals as the main character, Alex. The romantic drama included Irene Cara's song, "What a Feeling," which was still playing on the radio. I thought it was cool that Alex had a tomboy persona during the day and a sexy persona in the evening.

The second semester was coming to a close, with 30 days to go. I had my welding attire on. My persona wasn't as sleek as Jennifer Beals', but it was sexy cool. I was completing my arc welding assignment. Arc welding is when two pieces of metal are joined together with a heated torch. It was looking like a B grade. Then, I noticed in my peripheral vision a flashing light over my left shoulder. Then, the light was no longer flashing; it was a blaze of fire. My welding jacket had caught on fire. I totally forgot to stop, drop, and roll. I started slapping my shoulder and jacket. Then, I snatched that big-ass helmet off my face. The fire was finally out. So, the student helper, Jeff, stood there looking at me.

I said, "Did you see I was on fire?"

He said, "Yes, I knew you would handle it."

I said, "What the freak? I could've gone up in flames! Do we get to complete a survey about your assistance?"

The next few days, he greeted me when I arrived at class: "Hi, Adrienne."

I kindly rolled my eyes at him and went to my station.

The third day he greeted me: "Hi, Adrienne."

I said, "Hi, student assistant."

Then, we both laughed, and Jeff said, "You have dimples."

Then, I stopped smiling and went to my seat. Every day in class he initiated small talk that led to some conversations. Jeff had some intellect and a little swag. I liked our conversations because Jeff was attentive and engaged. On the other hand, his style of dress was just okay. Jeff wasn't a big talker, but he was socially observant and confident. When he talked, I leaned in and listened because it was going to be either something interesting or hilarious. As a typical high school boyfriend, Jeff looked pretty decent on paper. He was a junior, co-captain of the baseball team, had his own car, and worked some weekends doing welding jobs with his teacher. It was a week before summer break, and Jeff asked me out on a date.

I said, "Sure, assistant."

We talked on the phone a couple of times before he picked me up for our date. When he arrived, my friend Mary had just finished curling my feather cut hairstyle. I introduced him to my mom, my sisters Genia, Cheryl, and Nicky, and my friend Mary. We went go-kart racing and to the drive-in. The featured movie was *Bad Boys* and some kung fu movies. During the intermission, we compared the kung fu movie to the legendary *Enter the Dragon* with Bruce Lee, Jim Kelly, and Chuck Norris. The both of us enjoyed watching kung fu movies, especially *Samurai Sunday* on Channel 32 WFLD. The movie credits started rolling, and my eyes started to flutter. It was 10:30 p.m. and past my 9 p.m. bedtime. I slept from the time we were waiting to exit the drive-in until I arrived home 20 minutes later. Jeff walked me to my door. I thanked him for the date being the direct opposite of welding class and reassured him my sleepiness was not attributed to his company.

After our third date in a roll, Jeff asked if we could date exclusively. I said, "Sure."

The summer of 1984, we spent a lot of time at the 57th and Lake Shore Drive beach, "the Point." We also spent time at the boathouse behind the Museum of Science and Industry. People from various schools on the South Side, such as Simeon, Julian, and of course CVS, would listen to music and chill out on the lakefront. A couple of the hottest songs played on WGCI and WBMX radio stations were Lisa Lisa and Cult Jam's "I Wonder If I Take You Home" and Prince's "When Doves Cry." On another date, Jeff and I stood in a long line at Evergreen Plaza movie theater to see the sold-out legendary movie *Purple Rain*. It was worth the wait. One of the other places we liked to go was North Rush Street, one of the oldest and most popular streets in Chicago. Basically, high school students throughout Chicago would walk up and down the street like they were sightseeing and patronize restaurants, nightclubs, and record stores.

One of my favorite memories with Jeff is our Saturday mornings at Maxwell Street. It is notable as the location of the celebrated Maxwell Street Market, the birthplace of Chicago blues, and the "Maxwell Street Polish," a sausage sandwich. I also frequented it with my dad.

We went shopping, and the blues band on the southeast corner was jammin', playing "Muddy Water," "Hoochie Coochie Man," "Little Walter," "My Babe," and Bo Diddley tunes. Then, this guy asked us, "Would y'all like to buy the driving test with all the right answers?"

I said, "No, thank you."

He was such a persistent street vendor; he offered a couple more items. He asked, "How about a TV?"

In a humbled tone, I said, "No, thank you."

"Well, maybe you need a TV guide," he said.

Jeff said, "MAN, you not going to let us leave, are you? Damn, give us a pair of socks."

The guy said, "How about a pair for the young lady?"

Jeff said, "MAN, give me three pairs."

It was just another adventurous day on Maxwell Street. I swear it felt like we were in a scene from the TV show *Good Times*. Jeff and I laughed so hard. Jeff said, "I respect old boy's hustle."

Other enjoyable moments were conversations about Bible stories, such as 1 Samuel 17:32-33, where King David as a boy defeated the giant, Goliath. One famous statement uttered by elders in the black community, especially my mother growing up, referenced King David: "The bigger they are, the harder they fall." We were not biblical scholars or theologians, just two teenagers discussing how scriptures were interpreted in our community and family. Furthermore, the Book of Proverbs was and still is one of my favorite books in the Bible because it refers to wisdom as "She." Then I equated "she" with me as a black woman. Who knew that thought would lead me to become a black feminist? I highly suggested to Jeff to take heed of the word; it may just save his life one day. Jeff used to also sing a rendition of the Commodores' song "Jesus Is Love" acapella style. Those occasions drew me closer to him because he had a sense of maturity and could hold conversations of substance.

My dad thought Jeff was a respectful young man when they first met toward the end of the summer. Jeff exhibited all the southern traditions. As soon as he came into the house, he would address my dad with, "Yes, Sir. How are you doing?" He was charismatic and very well liked by my family. The summer came and went. It was time for me to usher in the 1984-85 school year as a sophomore and Jeff as a senior.

Geometry was a difficult subject for me. My algebra teacher fed me a falsehood: "You will do well in geometry since you understand the fundamentals of algebra." That was an absolute, absolute lie!

One day Jeff and some of his teammates were about to walk past my geometry class when Jeff made a sudden stop at the door. He said, "What's up, Mr. Cameron! My girlfriend is in this class; make sure she passes."

Mr. Cameron mumbled, "You have a girlfriend?" with a sarcastic undertone as only he could do. Another time, Mr. Cameron was standing in front of the chalkboard while lecturing about equilateral triangles (triangles with all sides equal and all angles equal). It's obvious geometry traumatized me for me to remember the lecture from 36 years ago.

One of the male students in the back of class said, "Mr. Cameron get your big ass out the way. You are blocking the board."

His mumbled comeback was, "Your mother has a big ass."

The students in front of class, including myself, looked at each other and giggled quietly. Thanks to Jeff tutoring me, I passed geometry with a high C, and I was elated. He dropped trigonometry in his junior year because it was boring, not from a lack of understanding.

Prom of '85

I thoroughly enjoyed accompanying Jeff to his Senior Prom as a sophomore. I wore a royal blue sleeveless line dress with a white mini birdcage veil. Jeff sported a white tuxedo with a royal blue cummerbund. The prom was held at Chicago Marriott Downtown

Magnificent Mile. The dance floor was full, like a black wedding reception minus the Cha Cha Slide. We attended two after-parties somewhere on the North Side. The prom festivities ended with a picnic at River Oaks Forest Preserve on Saturday and Marriott Six Flags in Gurnee, IL, on Sunday. Then it was time for the graduation festivities. The day of graduation, the class of '85 sang "We Are the World" and "It's So Hard to Say Goodbye to Yesterday" from the movie *Cooley High*. Black people sing "It's So Hard to Say Goodbye" like it's an old negro spiritual, or maybe it's just me. *Cooley High* is one of my favorite movies of all time. I still get choked up by the death of Cochise played by Lawrence Hilton-Jacobs, especially when Preach, played by Glynn Turman, arrived at Cochise's burial when everyone was leaving the cemetery. Preach read a poem to Cochise's grave and poured one (some wine into the grave) for his homie. Graduation night, we partied on the South Side, downtown, and the West Side of Chicago with Jeff's cousin, Kevin. It was time for the summer of 1985.

Fast Times @ Ford City Shopping Mall

F. W. Woolworth hired me for my first part-time job at Ford City Shopping Mall. I was a waitress and a cashier at Woolworth Grill located in the center of the mall. I worked every Thursday, Saturday, and Sunday evenings. The majority of my coworkers attended parochial schools. Myself and two others attended public schools. I'm still in disbelief that I was paid to play—I meant to say work—at the mall. My colleagues of various nationalities and I got along so well. We used to sing, dance, and joke before, during, and after work.

My colleague Mike tried to get someone to work his Saturday shift so he could go to Six Flags with friends. Unfortunately, no one was able to cover it. So, he forewarned us Friday night he had to call in sick and apologized for leaving us shorthanded. This particular Saturday, the restaurant manager, who didn't let anyone forget she had worked for F. W. Woolworth for 40 years, answered Mike's call instead of the managers who would have accepted diarrhea as a legitimate excuse. Oh no, the manager refused to let anyone get in the way of her $200 end of year bonus, even Mike and his uncontrollable bile. She told Mike there were plenty of restrooms he could use when needed. Mike told us what happened, and we couldn't stop laughing and joking about his restroom breaks.

Some Saturdays after work, some of us would go out to spend tips we earned and hang out even longer. The spring of 1986, I was promoted to a cook. Shortly after my promotion, I quit because the manager scolded me for refusing to take a banana out the trash can for a banana split. She said it was in good condition and just cut off the brown part. She insisted throwing away the banana would impact her bonus. I asked for a meeting with the store manager and the payroll clerk. I stated it was unsanitary and nasty to remove it from the trash and place it in the bowl, and I started crying and quit on the spot.

My mother became upset with me when I quit my job and even when I shared the reason why. I was like, "I'm 16 years old." Actually, I mumbled under my breath, "What the …" I didn't realize until some years later that she didn't want me to become comfortable with quitting. I went back and asked for my job back. I was welcomed with open arms. I felt like I hit the lottery when

I got my first paycheck. My dad had stopped my allowance the summer of 1985 and never put me back on Mr. Eugene Young's payroll as an unemployed teenager.

After graduation, Jeff attended a community college and tried out for the baseball team. Then he decided to go to the U.S. Army. He received an honorable discharge before he completed basic training. He didn't follow the drill sergeant's command and had an altercation with him because the sergeant had said something derogatory about Jeff's father. Then Jeff became ill. How convenient.

CHAPTER III

INVINCIBLE LOVE

Sr. Year Class of '87

At the beginning of my senior year of high school, things were starting to become a little chaotic at home. My parents were in the process of separating, so I left home and moved in with Jeff and his family. My mother and father were married for 24 years before separating for seven years. They divorced after 31 years of marriage. Personally, I was disappointed about the separation and the impact it had on our family's unity. Unfortunately, I wasn't surprised because I saw the wheels going off the rails a couple of years before. Nevertheless, I was optimistic and naive at the same time.

Before my mom married my dad, she was married to her high school sweetheart at the age of 16. My mom didn't get a chance to go to her senior prom because she was home "washing my older sister's cloth diapers and pregnant with my second sister." Also, during the 1950s, girls were not permitted to attend traditional high school and most definitely not to attend prom while pregnant. It was saddening for me to hear her teen years were spent being a young mother and a wife. She didn't graduate with her class of 1959 from DuSable High School. Eventually, my mom divorced her first husband and married my father. They were the parents of seven children: Jan, Cheryl, Gene, Genia, Dee Dee, Paddy (me), and Nicky. For most of her life, my mom was a stay-at-home mom, and she instilled in her six daughters the values, skills, and confidence that she wished she possessed for herself. Make no mistake, my mother was smart. She knew all the answers to the *Jeopardy* game show, and there were no reruns back then, so she legitimately knew the answers.

My mother was an avid reader. She loved to read autobiographies, black literature, and Unity's inspirational *Daily Word*. She wasn't afforded some opportunities without secondary school and collegiate attainment, which is why she was so adamant that all of her girls earned a college degree to help ensure our success wouldn't be predicated upon a man. Proudly, my mom received her General Educational Diploma (GED) in 2007. I loved my mother's direct communication style, also known as "straight, no chaser," meaning she didn't dilute her words. She could address any situation in a sophisticated manner. However, it bothered her if she had to address a situation in a sophisticated manner if it lacked sophistication.

Without realizing it at the time, my moving out was a gateway to future dysfunction. I never should've cohabited with my boyfriend at his mother's home at the age of 17. Jeff was 20 years old. Looking back on that experience, Jeff and I were pretending to be adults when the adults in our lives should've put us in our places.

During my senior year, I was an accounting major on the work-study program. The only place I was interested in being employed for work-study was Arthur Andersen, a firm that was one of the largest accounting firms in the United States at the time. After the third interview, I was told I was not selected as a work-study student at the prestigious firm. The news was so disappointing. So, I had to work about 30 hours per week at Burger King on 79th because my work-study teacher wouldn't accept my current job at F. W. Woolworth. I will never forget the experience at Burger King. All the managers were under the age of 27. Some of them behaved as if the restaurant was their personal playground. For example, they joked around when customers were present. The place was robbed on a weekly basis, only during the evening shift. Sadly, the environment was like crabs in a barrel, pulling each other down as anyone tried to get out. I thought if they're crabby at Burger King, I'd hate to see them in corporate America.

There were many perks of being on work-study. I acquired additional work experience and was dismissed from school at 11 a.m. In the meantime, I had to be dressed and in the gym room by 7 a.m. every day since I was on work-study. I was so ready for my senior year to be over. I wasn't hired for the position I longed for at the accounting firm. I didn't want to participate in any senior activities. My friend's boyfriend's mother made my prom dress the day before prom because I had no intention of going. The last-minute ivory-colored prom dress was gorgeous, and it complemented me well. Jeff and I attended my prom, but we didn't go to any after-parties because I was so tired from working so much. We did attend my class picnic. My friend Mary and her sister went with Jeff and me. I was having a nice time until Mary saw her son's father with his new girlfriend. Now, Mary's big mouth was the direct opposite of her 100- pound-soaking-wet figure. Let's just say, Mary caused a passive aggressive scene by going up to the couple and saying, "Hello" with a smirk.

Then, she pulled her son's father to the side and said, "Your new girlfriend looks like a fake Whitney Houston." After Mary's statement, he walked away, and they proceeded to mean-mug Mary with intense stares of disbelief and annoyance. Shortly before it was time to depart, Mary decided to plop on top of the cheap foam cooler purchased from Walgreens for $1.99. Even though she was only 100 pounds, all four sides of the foam cooler collapsed, and the few items left over were on the ground along with Mary. Looked like her son's father and the fake-looking Whitney Houston had the last laugh. As far as I know, that family never blended well.

I never purchased a class ring and didn't go on the senior trip to Florida. Overall, my senior year was stolen by misguidance and growing up too fast.

Another thing that was stolen was my childhood friend Michelle's life. She was the cousin of my long-time neighbor, Brian. We used to play on the block every time she visited Brian. Michelle was a senior at Dunbar Vocational High School and should have graduated with her classmates in June 1987. *The Chicago Defender* newspaper covered the heartbreaking story. In October 1986, Michelle's high school boyfriend murdered her with a gunshot to the head and then killed himself when she went over to his house to suggest they stop dating during their senior year. That was the first time I became aware of teen dating violence. My heart was broken, and I was in disbelief. Every now and then I think about Michelle and wonder what would have become of her life if she'd had the chance to live.

In spite of my unexpected senior year, I still kicked it and had loads of laughter. Sometimes Mary would pick me up from school when I didn't have to work so we could go to the mall and movies. Mary was two years older than me and had a son when she was 16 years old. She thought about joining the U.S. Army Reserves and attending Alabama State University. Then Mary started dating this guy who was a visiting recruiter for the U.S. Army. So, she invited me to go meet her new friend at the recruiting office. He was nice and looked like a typical guy in the armed forces. For instance, he had a physique like a gymnast and skin as smooth as a baby's bottom. As time progressed, Mary and her beau started double-dating with Jeff and me. The double-dating came to a halt once Mary's beau had to go to the Philippines.

Mary asked if I'd thought about attending Alabama State University with her after I graduated. I wasn't very familiar with the South, but I was open to a change of scenery. When I proposed the interesting idea to Jeff, he said, "Alabama is so far, and there are plenty of schools in Chicago." Without me realizing it then, Jeff was trying to assert control over my future. I decided to stay in Chicago with him.

Stork Introduction (1988)

Then, I ended up pregnant right after I graduated from high school. Our first child was due May 1988. In my first trimester of pregnancy, I was determined to work, so I went to work at

Schnakenberg Ace Hardware on the North Side of Chicago as a cashier. Every morning, I vomited on the train on my way to work for about two months. The morning sickness and nausea were unbearable, so I was bummed when I had to quit my job. By that time, I had started living between my parents' house and Jeff's mother's house. In addition, Jeff and I were in need of space. For no apparent reason, he started to hang out with some new friends at later hours than ever before. I also noticed Jeff was drinking more alcohol and smoking more weed. He was different, and I was pondering the next steps in my life.

Lo and behold, who came to visit my sister Cheryl while I was staying a couple of nights at my parents' house? The sizzle from the summer of '83. Unbeknownst to me, Eddie and Cheryl had stayed in touch. Cheryl went away to Northern Illinois University. Eddie went to the U.S. Army. It appeared that we both were stunned to see each other. We hadn't seen each other since the fall of 1984. He had grown approximately four to five inches. He still had a Jheri Curl, and it was styled like Johnny Gill, faded on the side with a circular part on the top right side. His voice was deeper, and he was still quite handsome, with a little more of everything.

Eddie asked, "How are you?"

I said, "Finer than you."

He chuckled, and we shared a slight grin. Then he said, "You let your hair grow longer, and you have a glow."

I said, "I'm pregnant."

He said, "I always liked your dimples. Can we go out to dinner to catch up?"

I said, with a side eye, "Sure."

Our first date as adults occurred the following week, when Eddie picked me up in his royal blue Pontiac Trans Am with T-tops that he rebuilt. As the evening unfolded, chivalry and fond memories of first love filled the air. That moment was like the final scene of the movie *Love Jones*, when Darius and Nina hadn't seen each other for quite some time. Before they leaned in for a kiss, he urgently confessed he still loved her. As sweet as that sounded from Eddie, I was pregnant with another man's child. We rode a carriage along Michigan Avenue in downtown Chicago. We ended the night with a warm, extended embrace and well wishes. Eddie said, "Call me anytime you need anything."

Then, I returned Jeff's call. I suggested to Jeff that we discuss our future concerning education, career, and our new residency. For the time being, he seemed like he was on board. He was working as a night security officer at an office building in downtown Chicago. In the meantime, my obstetrician/gynecologist at Michael Reese Hospital diagnosed my pregnancy as high-risk since I'd had a pregnancy loss the previous year. Michael Reese Hospital and Medical Center was known as a major research and teaching hospital and one of the oldest and largest hospitals in Chicago in the Bronzeville community. Prenatal visits bore resemblance to the reality TV shows *Basketball Wives* and the *Bad Girls Club*. The women in the waiting room sometimes would talk under their breath about each other, such as, "She needs to wear a bra" and "She's having another baby; this has to be her sixth one." My due date was June 5, 1988.

I was quite active during my full-term pregnancy. Sometimes I would babysit my nephew LaQuandus and my niece Stacy and take them to take pictures with the Easter bunny, to Lincoln Park Zoo, and out to Chuck E. Cheese. Jeff and I would go to the movies, go on Navy Pier boat cruises, and take walks along Chicago Lakefront Trail from 57th Lakeshore Drive to 31st Street Beach. Then again, plenty of times we didn't connect for days.

It was Friday, May 27th at approximately 1 a.m. I was talking to Jeff while he was at work and describing to him the painful movements in my stomach. I wasn't used to the aggressive kicks, only the cute little movements described in prenatal magazines at the doctor's office. The afternoon of Sunday, May 29th, on my way to my sister Cheryl's barbecue, I had difficulties walking and sitting at times, but the discomfort was manageable. Jeff assisted me the best he could throughout the time at Cheryl's barbecue. I told him he should just go to work. I would be okay. My family was there with several vehicles if they needed to transport me to the hospital. By 7 p.m., the contractions were coming every other hour. I did the breathing techniques I had read about. I was cool, calm, and collected. I couldn't let anyone see me sweat.

Most importantly, my nieces Shauntae and Stacy were starting to feel afraid for me. They continued to ask my sisters what's wrong with Aunt Paddy. I lay in my sister's mother-in-law's hospital bed at the house to try to relax, but it didn't work.

So, my dad and mom drove me to the hospital in a white and orange 1980 Chevy Van that didn't miss any potholes while en route. Immediately, I was taken to the labor and delivery wing. This time, the contractions were few and far between but were taking the wind out of me. The pain was excruciating. I had never felt throbbing, discomfort, agony, torture, soreness, aching, agony, and nausea all at the same time. It was so bad, I said "agony" twice. My mother was in the room with me when the nurses arrived to connect me to the tocodynamometer to monitor the frequency and length of my contractions. Up to this point, the contractions were about 30 minutes apart, but the nurse said, "Contractions should be at least 5-10 minutes apart in order to prepare for labor and delivery."

I kindly said, "Pardon me?"

The nurse said, "Yes, Ms. Young, your contractions aren't close enough, and you don't seem like you are in that much pain."

Now, remember I was cool, calm, and collected for my nieces. I read that it was best for my body and my baby to stay relaxed. In the back of my mind, while trying to relax, I thought, "Did she read the same materials the OB-GYN shared with me?" and "Is she for real?"

Then, the nurse sent me home because of "false" labor pains, also known as Braxton Hicks contractions. My mother and I were in disbelief that I was sent home. Unfortunately, this was my first experience with black maternal health disparities.[6] The harrowing pain described was dismissed because I "didn't seem like I was in that much pain." But there's a bigger problem: There are many stories about how historically black women are not monitored as carefully as white women, and their complaints are dismissed. My father drove me 10 miles back to my mom's house in Englewood. It was me, my mom, my dad, and the potholes again. My dad dropped me and my mom off at home about 10 p.m. I kid you not, I walked into the house and needed to go to the bathroom, and before I could go, my water bag burst. Remember, it was 1988 and cell phones were not as popular for everyday people like me and my parents. So, I had to wait until my dad arrived at his place on the East Side, approximately 5 miles away. My sister Nicky called our dad on the landline phone to tell him to turn right back around to pick me up to go back to the hospital. Nicky and Mom arrived back at the hospital with me at roughly 11:30 p.m., and the same nurse who discharged me greeted me with a "Hello."

The dysfunctional labor began at 11:45 p.m. It's also known as dystocia, meaning abnormally slow progress. My labor progress was as slow as the three-toed sloth, which is considered the slowest mammal in the world. The nursing staff asked me several times if I wanted an epidural. I was totally against someone inserting a long-ass needle in my spine. I'm very protective of my spine and eyes. I can't live without them. I had nightmares that the person designated to inject the needle would cough, sneeze, or have a need to scratch some part of their body and cause permanent nerve damage. So, I endured.

Water was prohibited; only ice chips were given to me from 11:45 p.m. until Jeff arrived at 8 a.m. May 30th. He asked for a washcloth so he could soak it with cold water to put on my forehead. Instead, he squeezed the cold water into my mouth. I felt some relief with actual water as opposed to ice chips. Then, the contractions were coming as fast as lightning. I started hyperventilating as fast as the contractions. Next, Jeff started singing the Commodores' "Jesus Is Love" in my ear. Eventually, I became cool, calm, and collected again. I was ready to meet my baby in person for the first time. Earlier in my pregnancy, I had decided not to seek out the gender of my baby.

Hence, it was time for delivery. I was fed another falsehood: Delivery is less painful than labor. My delivery was dry, since my water bag had burst 13 hours earlier, so I had to push a baby without any fluids. The dry delivery ended with an episiotomy and 30 stitches. My firstborn, Taja Ciara Spires, arrived at 1:16 p.m. and weighed 7 pounds and 8 ounces. It was the same year as Chicago's infamous 1988 summer drought. Taja had a green birthmark that started from the upper right side of her ear lobe down to her rosy cheek line. She had thick, curly black hair and slightly slanted dark brown eyes. After the long wait to meet Taja, I was finally happy to meet my healthy baby girl.

Reaching for Higher Ed

Early into motherhood, I was totally unaware of what postpartum depression was. I didn't know any of the characteristics or symptoms, but I do recall being socially withdrawn, kind of moody, and sad. Looking back, I was disappointed that we were starting a family so soon instead of attending college together somewhere, actually anywhere. So, I decided to enroll in a six-month program at a for-profit school, The Computer Learning Center in downtown Chicago. I earned a certification in Word Perfect, Lotus 1-2-3 Spreadsheets, and dBase management. I never should've gone to a for-profit school because the cost was astronomical and the benefits were insignificant. Then I worked for a couple of temporary agencies for about two years and was assigned some long-term assignments, for instance with the Chicago Public Health Department. However, nothing led to a permanent position.

The certification didn't work out as I thought. Then I enrolled at Richard J. Daley College, a community college of Chicago, to major in accounting. Unexpectedly, Illinois Bell Telephone

Company and First Chicago Bank called me to interview for full-time employment opportunities. I turned down interviews and decided to just go to a real college full-time. I knew that I needed a degree so I could become more marketable. To my dismay, I had to take English 100 instead of 101. Actually, being in the 100-level course helped me remember some fundamentals and concepts I didn't remember from elementary and secondary school.

Daley College had a daycare on campus for students and staff, and I was able to enroll Taja full-time, which was great. If you could have your child go to school with you, and most definitely in a university or college setting, it's like having the best of both worlds because children are being exposed to student teachers who are majoring in early childhood education under the supervision of a licensed teacher. As a parent, I was able to monitor Taja during class via the observation room with a two-way glass mirror and an audio device to hear what was being said in class. Taja and I enjoyed the extracurricular activities and class trips the daycare hosted.

I was a work-study student and worked part-time in the computer lab for about three semesters. Vermeil was the office manager, and her office was the hangout spot. The first time I met Vermeil, or I thought it was the first time, she came up to me while I was standing in the financial aid line and said, "Hi, my name is Vermeil. I remember when you were a little girl."

I said, "Say what?"

Then she giggled and told me she used to be a member of my mother's Girl Scout Troop when she was younger. That was the start of a new friendship. Vermeil introduced me to some outgoing sistas. We had some of the best conversations in her office about things such as dating and marriage and our career aspirations, and we also talked and sang songs. I had fun with other classmates as well. We had a couple of classes together and hung out during and after class. One of my favorite professors at Daley College was Professor Roundtree who taught Business Law 102. He often laughed at my moral compass during class discussions. For example, he said, "Oh, Adrienne, you would do well in a moral court, but law has absolutely nothing to do with morals." Then Professor Roundtree would release a mischievous and rasping laugh like the famous animated dog Muttley from Hanna-Barbera Productions. In spite of the snickering, I really liked the content and his lectures.

Stork Visit (1991)

Shockingly, in the spring semester of 1991, I had an unexpected visit from a tall, long-legged wading bird with a long, heavy bill and typically with white and black plumage: the stork. So, I continued to strive as a full-time student and worked in the business office for the work-study program until the end of the year. By the summer, Jeff suggested we relocate to Champaign-Urbana, IL, to enroll in Parkland College. He planned to major in Tool and Die. I planned on transferring to the University of Illinois Champaign-Urbana campus to major in accounting, especially since Arthur Andersen heavily recruited students from the School of Accounting and Business. Jeff had earned a certificate in Machinery from Dawson Community College and was a machinist at a company on the North Side of Chicago. The arrangement was to live with Jeff's friend and his wife for about six months until we moved into our own place.

It was December 19th, and I decided to spend the night at my mother's house. I was pooped when I arrived at about 6 p.m. I got in bed with my mother and was watching television, or the TV was watching me. I woke up several times to go to the restroom. I sat straight up in the bed at 4:45 a.m. I went to the bathroom again and again. The pain ushered its way into my lower back, and my leg went numb. Since the second trimester, this baby had a habit of lounging on my pelvis. Sometimes, I walked with a limp that made it appear like I had a fake leg. It wasn't very becoming for a 22-year-old young mother-to-be. It was all good after I did a couple of stretches, and I went back to bed. Oddly, I didn't want to go to the hospital too early after my first birth experience.

My mother woke up and said, "When did you get here?"

I said, "Last night." She didn't realize I'd slept with her.

She asked, "Are you okay?"

Nonchalantly, I said, "I'm in labor. I just took a shower, and I'm going to wait a little longer before I leave."

My mother: "WHY THE HELL would you get in the shower while you're in labor!"

I said, "I need to be fresh and relaxed."

My mama yelled, "Get your relaxed ASS to the hospital!"

Strangely, all of a sudden, the labor pains started coming. My siblings Gene and Cheryl heard my scream and came to my mother's room. I had a towel wrapped around me because I was about to put on my cocoa butter and pull my hair into a ponytail. My breathing was faint.

Mama said, "Get her dressed!"

They were trying to put on my clothes. I called for my sister Nicky. She ran down the stairs, and I said, "Please look in my book bag and find my papers so I can get my tubes tied."

Mama said, "They should have it on file at the hospital!"

I said, "I can't go without it!"

Then we realized Gene's car was in the shop. Jeff was on the Northside, and my dad didn't answer his landline phone. So, Nicky ran across the street to our friend to take us to the hospital. I believe Nicky caught Lisa in the nick of time because she was getting in her car. Gene and Cheryl helped me to the car. I looked like a hot mess. I had on one sock, some sweatpants, no underwear, a T-shirt, and my mother's blue jean coat about as big as an old overcoat. They totally disregarded the clothes I laid out to wear per my mother's curt and direct orders. Growing up, my mother always told my siblings and I to wear clean underwear and matching socks whenever we go out of the house. Those values were nowhere to be found, literally.

Finally, we made it to the car. Nicky handed me my signed documents to get a tubal ligation (tube tie). I held the papers close to me. We arrived in the parking lot at Chicago Osteopathic Hospital located in Hyde Park at 7:10 a.m. Nicky ran into the hospital to get me a wheelchair. I got out of the car and started taking off the coat and my clothes with one hand while holding my papers in the other because my body felt like a furnace, and I was sweating like I'd just run a marathon.

Lisa started screaming, "Paddy, what are you doing?"

At last Nicky arrived with the wheelchair. Then she asked, "Why the hell are you out here in this parking lot damn near naked?"

Once Nicky rolled me into the hospital, the staff transported me to the labor and delivery ward at 7:15 a.m. I handed the nurse my papers to give to the doctor. I was given some excuse that the documents weren't on file long enough. My baby, who was expected on December 28th, arrived on December 20th at 7:25 a.m. Tonja Natasha Spires was exactly 6 pounds.

After Tonja was born, the nurse said, "If you had lived about two more blocks west, you would've delivered your baby in the parking lot."

CHAPTER IV

NEW BEGINNINGS: CHAMBANA

Jeff went to Champaign, Illinois the day after Christmas. I boarded the Greyhound bus to Champaign with an 11-day-old baby and 3½-year-old on New Year's Eve. We wanted to bring in the New Year in our new place of residency. My parents were not pleased with me moving with a newborn and a toddler on the bus. I was young and eager for new possibilities.

Tee and Sandy had a nice three-bedroom house in Southwest Champaign. They had one son, Terrence Jeffrey, "TJ." Tee and Jeff made a pact when they were younger. They would name their sons after each other and become the godfathers. I told both of them I thought that was an honorable pact, however, I wasn't part of it. So, if Jeff and I were to ever have a son, his first name wouldn't be Terrence. Most importantly, I made a pact with the stork: No more visits.

Jeff and I got along really well and had some of the most thought-provoking conversations about entrepreneurship, education, and religion. Sometimes, we watched Bishop TD Jakes' sermons after Les Brown, the motivational speaker. Once we put the kids to sleep, we also watched Def Comedy Jam on Friday nights. May he continue to rest in peace; Bernard Jeffrey McCullough, better known as Bernie Mac, hands down was one of the best comedians on Def Jam and Kings of Comedy. The comedic line that led him to fame was "I ain't scared of you mutha****," and he did his infamous hip-hop dance moves after his punchline and then would say, "kick a**." In addition, my admiration is partial to Bernie Mac because we're both from the South Side of Chicago and alumni of Chicago Vocational High School.

Jeff and I set a timeline to move into our own apartment and enroll part-time at Parkland in August. Unfortunately, that plan wasn't possible for me since my student loan went into default. Daley College's business office didn't submit my deferment forms to the Department of Education. Consequently, a contingency plan was needed, and fast. I saw that mishap as an opportunity to better prepare for the future we envisioned for our family. Later, I recalled what one of my accounting professors had said, "It's good to reside in a college town since they tend to have a strong economy even if the overall economy is struggling. Because rich people will always send their children to college." Next, I thought, easy-peasy, let's roll. I was ready to grow in so many other areas in my life until I rebooted my collegiate studies, such as motherhood, spirituality, health, and with my future husband.

Jeff worked the third shift at Solo Cup Company on the assembly line. Shortly after his hire, he worked in the machinery department on a trial basis. He wasn't hired for the machinist position after the three-month trial period. The girls and I were asleep before Jeff left for work. My babies and I were on a good and consistent sleeping schedule. We went to sleep at about 8:30 p.m., not later than 9 p.m. Going to sleep early was never a problem for me; some people referred to it as "beauty rest." For as long as I could remember, my eyes started to flutter about 8 p.m. I was just tired.

When the spring approached, I put Taja and Tonja in the stroller and walked around Kaufman Lake every morning for an hour and prayed and sang gospel songs such as, "His Eye Is On the Sparrow." Then we sat on the deck at the lake and fed the ducks and fish. Periodically, Jeff would join us when he got off work and before he went to bed. I thoroughly enjoyed being a mother and reading and singing nursery rhymes and rhythm and blues (R&B) with my girls. One time I passed the mic to Taja and she started singing the Jackson 5 rendition of the James Brown song, "I Got the Feelin." Our favorite part was "baby, baby, baby." My nephew LaQuandas used to have belly laughs when I sang it to him when he was about a year old. As a family we were really starting to come together. Jeff and I had collective goals accompanied with romance.

Before we knew it, summer had arrived. The girls, TJ, and I fancied Sholem Aquatic Center at Centennial Park about three times a week. In July 1992, the girls and I left for Chicago for the remainder of the summer to hang out with family and friends. Jeff stayed behind to work two jobs to earn additional cash to prepare for our move. We had a blast while in Chicago with both sides of the family. My mother hosted the annual Fourth of July celebration/family birthday party.

Time to share a little-known black history fact. Black people in America, especially my family, were fully aware that our ancestors' independence didn't take place on July 4, 1776. The Emancipation Proclamation went into effect January 1, 1863, and freed the enslaved native Black Americans. Yet, the barbaric Texas legislators and slave owners and other powers neglected to share the memo from President Abraham Lincoln that slavery was abolished on January 1, 1863. The message wasn't communicated until June 19, 1865, two and a half years later. The act was so brutish, "Juneteenth" has become a day to commemorate the end of slavery. The Fourth of July was celebrated as a day off with pay for birthday celebrations and barbecues. You often hear the barbecue theme song, "Got to Give It Up" by Marvin Gaye, from 1977 to the present. My Aunt Cookie's husband, Anthony, was the DJ. The celebration entailed card games, dancing, singing, eating, fireworks (just for fun), and various conversations. As I previously shared, "Ain't No Party Like a South Side Party."

When it was time to return to Champaign, I enrolled Taja at Marquette Champaign Early Childhood Center. She attended three hours Monday through Friday. Taja was so excited when the bus arrived; she told Tonja, "I can't play with you now. I must go to school," and kissed her on her forehead. We all laughed, and then Jeff walked Taja to the school bus. Tonja and I greeted Taja every day when she got off the bus.

Meanwhile, I started working at the Country Fair movie theater on Saturdays and Sundays from 11 a.m. to 11 p.m. to earn some extra money so we could move because we were a month behind our target date. Soon after, we moved into a two-bedroom and half bath townhouse at Scotts Wood Manor in Urbana, an income-based property. Our new home was cozy and full of love. Jeff was able to walk to work at Solo Cup. He had to walk approximately two blocks.

Mama Dreamt of Fish

One day, my mother called me to share that her mother, Mama Sarah, had a dream about fish. Let me give a brief disclaimer about fish swimming in dreams. In the black community, such dreams are viewed as an old wife's tale, an African proverb, superstitions, and some truth. Whenever a black mother or grandmother dreams about fish, someone in the family is destined to be pregnant. So, my mom has six daughters and called all of us and said, "Oh my goodness, Sarah had a dream about fish." The atmosphere felt like a scene from the television show *Cold Case*, where the detectives tried to uncover new evidence for an unsolved investigation. Guess what? I had the little guppy swimming in Mama Sarah's dream. I said, "I told that darn stork, no more visits!"

CHAPTER V

HONEYMOON PHASE

Third Stork Visit Was a Charm, 1992?

When we moved, the stork tapped me on my shoulder for the third time to let me know I would meet my third bundle of joy in seven months. The third time's a charm, right? Once again, those indescribable feelings resurfaced, and I became a little withdrawn from my daily routine and felt sad for no apparent reason. I longed for adult conversation. I was at home with a toddler, Tonja, and a preschooler, Taja, watching *Barney* and *Gullah Gullah Island* and singing nursery rhymes on a daily basis. Jeff was working two jobs, and when I arrived home, I had only enough energy to talk for about 30 minutes. We were new tenants at Scottswood Manor, and I only waved to a couple of my neighbors when I entered and departed my unit. Most of my adult interaction was talking to my sister, DD, and my sister-in-law, Shirley, on the telephone. I really just wanted to get out of the house.

So, I'm pregnant with my third child. My children's godmother, Sandy, informed me Parkland College was offering scholarships for single mothers to enroll in two classes or up to six credit hours. The scholarship paid for both courses and one book. My sister Dee Dee paid for the other book. I enrolled in English 101 and a Women's Studies course. The girls stayed home with Jeff whenever I went to class. Both courses were intriguing. I had opportunities to have collegiate, cultural, and social conversations.

I recall one evening in my Women's Studies class, Professor Pauline Kay led a discussion about women's menstrual cycles and birth pain and said, "We can thank Eve for all that." I knew Eve was blamed for Adam eating the forbidden fruit, but I thought, can she get a break, or maybe Adam could've taken one for the team, sweet Jesus. Then, Professor Kay had the class read stories and essays written by women. The two women who stood out the most were Phillis Wheatley and Virginia Woolf. Ms. Wheatley was a poet who was enslaved in America and earned her freedom. Most importantly, she was the first African American and enslaved person and the third woman to have her first published poems in 1767 and 1773. She wrote poems on various subjects, religion, and morals. She shared that before she was enslaved in America, her family resided in Senegal/Gambia and were members of the Muslim faith.

As an abolitionist, Phillis Wheatley thought the American Revolution would also offer freedom to enslaved Africans since America was fighting for their freedom from Great Britain while using some enslaved African men. As I pondered on the discussion, I found it ironic that it was 1993, and black soldiers were fighting in the Gulf War, also known as Desert Storm, and still weren't free from systemic racism and police brutality. And in the previous year, 1992, Rodney King's beating had been captured on video.

Virginia Woolf's essay, "A Room of One's Own," published in 1929, emphasized, "A woman must have money and a room of her own if she is to write fiction." I favor Woolf's suggestion that "the absence of female fiction is a result of a lack of opportunity rather than a distinct absence of talent." During the class discussion, I redirected the conversation from Virginia and all of her peers, who brought awareness to inequality and patriarchy that wouldn't allow them to unveil their intellect. This essay was written 16 ½ years after the Women's Suffrage March (March 3, 1913) and nine years after the 19th Amendment (August 26, 1920) was enacted so women could have the right to vote. These dates are notable because black women had formed state chapters that helped plan and execute the Suffrage March. For example, Ida B. Wells-Barnett was cofounder of the Illinois Chapter Alpha Suffrage Club.

Consequently, the Illinois Chapter was told to march at the end of the line. Ida B. Wells refused and walked in front of the line. I'm sharing all this to shed light on the fact that black women's fight for justice and equality and to display their intellectual capital has been ongoing for multiple decades, if not centuries. During the dialogue, I thought about black women who were able to write fiction and nonfiction books, newspaper articles, and poems without some of the luxuries and privileges, such as Gwendolyn Brooks, poet and Pulitzer Prize winner, and

Lucy Parson, founder of the *Freedom* newspaper addressing the lynching of black men.

I will also never forget the intriguing English 101 class. During the 1992 presidential election, Bill Clinton, Ross Perot, and George H. W. Bush were the hot topics in class discussions. For example, the expected impact each candidate would have on college students if elected. The question I posed was, "Why is it that everyone is so excited about Bill Clinton, good grief?" The black community was elated with Bill and went as far as calling him the first black president. I was like, what and why? Is it because he played the saxophone with dark sunglasses on the Arsenio Hall Show? Unfortunately, none of my classmates took a stab at my questions. I wondered if it was because I was the only black person in the class.

On the contrary, the black community was heavily impacted by saxophone Bill's full support of the crime bill that decimated black communities and added to the pipeline to historic incarceration and the 1994 North American Free Trade Agreement (NAFTA). I recall asking my daddy his thoughts about NAFTA, and he stated it would take away jobs that paid above a living wage, especially union jobs. And if union jobs are shipped outside of America, unions won't be able to advocate for fringe benefits, such as medical, pension, and paid vacation. Our discussion was very insightful.

I was doing quite well in both classes. Then, I went into preterm labor and had to withdraw. My daughter, Tesha, was born May 28, 1993, instead of June 11th. She weighed exactly five pounds. When Tesha was approximately four months old, I returned to the workforce.

Bank One hired me as a part-time teller for the 4 p.m. to 12 a.m. shift. By then, Jeff worked from 5:30 a.m. to 1:30 p.m. in the hospital cafeteria. We worked opposite schedules to avoid high daycare costs. Jeff did not want anyone to watch his daughters, so he stayed home with them.

Inaugural Marriage Conference & Nuptial

Bank One was a sponsor for Champaign's Black Expo, and I signed up to volunteer at the booth at Douglas Center located at the north end of town, where a large percentage of African Americans resided. I have to admit I was a little taken aback that the Black Expo was so small because, in Chicago, the Expo was humongous. There would be thousands of people and hundreds of vendors, just a lot of black love. It was a pleasure to meet Mrs. Bridges, stationed at the Bank One booth to introduce a housing program funded by Bank One's Community Reinvestment Act (CRA). Mrs. Maryanne invited Jeff and me to her church home, Living Faith Ministries.

Bishop Abe Richardson was the presiding pastor, and his wife, Sister Richardson, was the co-pastor. We became official members in the spring of 1994. Church service was held in the basement of the YWCA building on the University of Illinois Champaign-Urbana campus.

Bishop Richardson invited Jeff and me to our inaugural Marriage Conference in the summer of 1994. We were cohabiting with our three daughters, and I believe that was one of the main reasons we received an invitation. In addition, we were thinking about getting married, especially since we were "living in sin"—basically, we were playing house without the appropriate marriage license. I recall having wholesome conversations with the couple who provided janitorial services at Bank One during my break.

One night, the wife asked, "When will you and Jeff get married?"

I said, "I'm not sure."

She said, "Let me share something with you. A man has to have a license for his dog and to make sure he's committed to you as the woman in his life and the mother of his children."

I wasn't offended by her statement by any means. I figured we had been "shacking up" for about six years. She stressed the point of commitment and responsibilities. Jeff and I were looking forward to the conference. I wanted to see what a healthy marriage is supposed to look like from a spiritual standpoint and what we have to do for our marriage to be successful.

We took the girls to Jeff's sisters, Ann and Jackie, in Chicago to babysit while we attended the Marriage Conference held at the Illini Union back in Champaign. Jeff and I were in the company of couples married for at least 10 years, and some marriages were between 25 and 30 years old. One activity we thoroughly enjoyed was the marriage trivia game, where we had to answer questions about each other. For example, the "Love You When" game is where each spouse writes down everything they love about each other in five minutes. The couple with the most love items wins, and the couples agree on the same pet name for their spouse. We most definitely got our sizzling pet names correct, and we refused to share it in public with our spiritual elders. Scriptures that spoke about the foundation of marriage and the roles God assigned to husbands and wives were discussed throughout the retreat, such as Proverbs 18:22, *"He who finds a wife finds what is good and receives favor from the LORD."* The book of Proverbs is one of my favorites because wives help their husbands with God's favor, and wisdom refers to her.

Conference members traveled to Chicago for an early dinner at Michael Jordan's restaurant and attended Monument of Faith Evangelist Church, where Rev. R. D. Henton was the senior pastor. We were in for a real treat. Bishop Barbara Amos, founder of Faith Deliverance Christian Center, Inc. from Norfolk, Virginia, was the guest speaker, and gospel singer Donnie McClurkin was the guest singer. My bonus maternal grandmother Kay served in the choir for approximately 40 years.

After the four-day conference, we felt renewed and ready to prepare for our marriage. I figured our marriage had a chance as long as we worked as a team. On the way to pick up the girls, we discussed the household budget, continuing education, purchasing a home in the near future, and getting ready to say our vows. We were convinced to get new pet names after all the talk about wedding vows and love.

CHAPTER VI

WET BEHIND THE EARS (TENSION-BUILDING PHASE)

Jeff and I were still riding high from the marriage conference we'd attended. Knowing we were entering a new phase in our relationship, from cohabiters to husband and wife, was reassuring. We had an informal wedding ceremony at Bishop Richardson and Sister Richardson's home on July 8, 1994.

The reality of adulthood puts any and all illusions to rest. I said to Jeff that our parents had a total of 15 children between the four of them, and not one of them had a high school diploma. They were homeowners who could supply all the essential needs for their families. So, we had no excuse not to do the same and more for our family. We were in total agreement and set out to conquer our plan.

Approximately three months later, I realized Jeff's enthusiasm and work attendance had started to dwindle. I noticed he was becoming moody and anxious. These behaviors were unfamiliar to me. It wasn't just due to a few cocktails here or there or marijuana. Sadly, he started doing crack cocaine, and that bothered me because I knew that it was addictive. It's 1994, and we saw what happened in the late '80s in Chicago. Black communities throughout the United States were decimated by crack cocaine. The term "crackheads" was a descriptor for the people hooked on drugs, and babies were born addicted. Some black men and women were prostituting themselves to get a hit.

Say No to Drugs, I Wish!

So, when I confronted Jeff about smoking crack again, he denied it. This confrontation made me think about one of my dad's life lessons. We were watching the movie *The Godfather*, the scene where about 20 mob bosses were sitting around a huge table voting if they should add the sale of drugs to their repertoire of gambling and prostitution. The deal was sealed when all agreed no drugs were to be sold in their communities and only to the "fucking molies" (i.e., black people). I was about seven years old when this was brought to my attention. Jeff and I had this conversation on more than one occasion. I didn't understand why he subjected himself to the poison dropped intentionally in our community.

Then, he finally confessed to it and said, "I don't do it that much, and it's not as addictive as people think."

What kind of bull crap response was that? He had figured we would leave Chicago so he could start over in a new environment, Champaign. He had pitched the idea of relocating to Champaign for a new start. The start was more for him than for us. He preferred to run from the so-called temptation instead of treating the addiction. He had a similar analogy for people being released from jail not to return to the community that influenced the behavior that got them in trouble. This had nothing to do with his environment; this had to do with his addiction, his selfishness of knowing that he had a family to contribute to but wanted to continue to do drugs. I didn't even know all the signs; there were times he was just drinking way more than usual. And I was totally unaware of what was causing him to drink more, and I later found out drinking helped curb his craving for crack cocaine.

And this is when the domestic disputes started. I would stress to Jeff, "You need to take better care of yourself. We have kids to raise 'together.' This is not why we came down to Champaign, Illinois. We had a team plan, and we needed to execute it immediately."

Jeff didn't want to hear anything I had to say. He felt I was nagging him and he was going to handle it. Whatever that meant.

I was thinking to myself, okay, you know what to do. I'm not smoking any damn crack. I was like, what needs to be done? I had a team mentality. I was thinking about the purpose of attending the marriage conference that he wanted to attend.

"Okay, I'm not going to use it anymore," he said, and he stopped using it. He started going back to work on time and contributed to savings for about three months. Low and behold, another relapse. I wish giving up drugs was just as easy as saying no to drugs.

During this time, Jeff's behavior was erratic, such as making illogical statements. He was offensive and very defensive at the same time. I know that sounds like an oxymoron, but if anyone could pull it off it was Jeff. He was accusatory; he felt like I was doing things behind his back and not supportive of him.

Jeff shouted, "I would die for you!"

But I had to tell him, "Negro, I need you to live for me and our three daughters; that's not sexy at all."

Jeff was always willing to die for us, while I was trying to live for us.

Hello 911

Consequently, these two philosophical actions can't make for a happy home because living requires more determination and discipline! I totally understood Jeff's attempt to convey the depths of his love for me through death. However, I needed that depth in the living, not the dead.

He wasn't happy with our exchange, so he hit me, and I hit him back. I wasn't afraid. I said, "You know, I don't have a problem with fighting back."

Another time, we had a very explosive dispute. You talk about tension building. He was busy telling me how he didn't like the fact that I would use the word "with" instead of "wit," and that I thought I was better than him.

I asked, "How is using standard English putting you down?"

He had no answer to my question. Mind you, I wasn't spending money on Gucci or Prada. I never lived above my means. If anything, I had to live beneath because the expense of Jeff and his addictions surpassed his income. I knew that we were in the beginning stages of building, and we should never despise small beginnings, but Jeff didn't see it that way.

Wet Behind the Ears (Tension-Building Phase)

One particular night, I had to call 911 because Jeff didn't "like the way" I responded to him, and he started strangling me. After I bathed and put the kids to bed, he came into the house and accused me of talking to a man at the back window.

I said, "So you supposedly stood and watched me talk to a fictitious man instead of ensuring your family was okay. You should've had your ass in the house helping with these kids."

The last thing I wanted was to get the police involved in our lives. We were black adults born and raised in black communities and knew some police involvement didn't come with positive outcomes. The last thing I ever wanted was for my children to wake up and find me dead on the living room floor. I valued my life and being in our children's lives. But I dialed 911. While Jeff was being arrested, he shouted to me, "Pat, you going to let them arrest me?"

I refused to respond. One of the officers asked if me and the girls would be okay. "Yes, we will. Thank you for asking."

During that time, the District Attorney's office had the power to press charges against the perpetrator in domestic violence disputes. The option to press charges was totally out of the hands of the victim. This procedure was a way to protect the victim from being placed in a compromising position. Jeff was looking at serving about 1-2 years in prison or on probation.

Tee recommended an attorney to Jeff. His attorney was able to come to an agreement with the DA. The deal consisted of a misdemeanor charge, a court-ordered domestic violence treatment program, and anger management classes, as well as supervised probation for 12 months. In addition, Jeff had to pay court fees and the cost of the mandatory classes. The total cost was roughly $1,200. I agreed he could return home after enrolling in the treatment program.

During the first couple of weeks, Jeff didn't really want to share anything about the class content. I let him have his space. The class was difficult for him since he preferred to be in control even though he had the inability to manage several aspects of life, such as by overindulging in drugs and drinking and lacking the discipline to hold a job consistently and managing family responsibilities. After the fourth week, Jeff opened up about his classes and stated that he was learning much about himself.

I asked, "How so?"

He said, "I need to focus on being a family man, accept the responsibilities of being a man of the house, and figure out ways to control my anger."

He believed or was coached to believe the anger came from drugs and alcohol. I was puzzled by the analogy. Now, I was no substance abuse counselor or sponsor for Alcoholics Anonymous (AA). However, it appeared once again he was passing the buck and not taking any responsibility for his actions.

As time progressed, he shared the interactions between himself and other males in the class. They became like accountability buddies. They liked the facilitators' nonjudgmental approach and that the men were able to disclose with support. In addition, the instructors brought much needed attention to the negative impact of the over usage of substances and alcohol. Eventually, Jeff fulfilled the necessary requirements ordered by the court.

Wet Behind the Ears (Tension-Building Phase)

After counseling, he decided he was going to try to stop drinking and doing drugs. He was on the sobriety train, and hopefully, he wouldn't fall off. Actually, in the back of my mind, I thought I wished him the best, but could he handle cold turkey? The abrupt halt from drugs and alcohol was a serious attempt. Throughout his sobriety efforts, I supported him by engaging in activities with him, such as the girls and me walking on the track while he jogged, watching him play basketball at Hessel Park, and other ventures. The old Jeff was resurfacing. We were becoming friends again. Fortunately, the sobriety moment was doable. It was time for us to huddle up and regroup as a team. As a team, we were going to work together. So, I shared with him what I didn't want to happen in this team effort. For example, he's in the dugout while I'm on the field, and he's pointing out the balls that need to be picked up. Then I said, "I don't want to be on a team like that."

Finally, we were getting back on track. Jeff was working consistently at the hospital from 5:30 a.m. to 1 p.m. I was unemployed and stayed home with the girls. I continued to take on the role of a wife. I cooked seven days a week. Jeff was accustomed to eating home-cooked meals, and I was used to it a little bit. For instance, on Friday nights, we ate fried fish, spaghetti with meat sauce, coleslaw, and/or garden salad, and on Saturdays, we ate homemade pizza or tacos. Some Sundays, I made butter beans with ham hocks or turkey legs, cornbread, fried chicken, and caramel cake with homemade caramel. Jeff was still sober and free of substances. A budget was set, and we stuck with it for three months.

We were doing quite well in almost all the areas of our lives and riding on the love train again. Next, I had to go to Chicago to visit my paternal aunt, Annie, who was stricken with cancer. Shortly after my visit, she passed away. That was devastating for me, since I loved her so much. Her funeral was almost 10 years to the day from that of her mother, our grandmother, Mama. I used to spend at least two weekends per month during the school year and some weeks during summer break at her house up until I was about 14 years old. She was an amazing cook and she baked the best homemade cakes, such as coconut and pineapple and yellow cake with homemade chocolate icing. I have to credit her for my interest in jazz music. On Sunday morning, she was listening to jazz on the radio and I changed the station. She said, "Who turned the radio station?" Then, I had to fess up, or maybe my twin cousins, Karen and Keith, would tell on me.

So, I said, "I did." That was the only time she ever scolded me. It took some time for me to appreciate her scolding because I was introduced to another form of music invented by black Americans. That was a sad experience for me because she had never raised her voice to me, but I had it coming.

I recall having an adult conversation with Annie when I was 22 years old. One day, I decided to stop by to say hello. We began to talk about school, family, and dating. She gave me one piece of advice that stuck with me, but I didn't use it when I first had the chance. She said, "Don't let anyone mistreat you, especially not a man who is supposed to love you."

The Stork Returns with Two Gifts, '95

When I returned home in December, I went to the doctor's office for a pregnancy test. I knew I was pregnant, but I didn't want to face it. After the test revealed I was with child, my obstetrician-gynecologist had the nurse and technician prep me for an ultrasound to verify the trimester. I gave permission for a medical student to be present during the ultrasound. Throughout the time, I lay on the cold examining table in a comatose state. What caused me to become alert was the loud, excited roar from the medical student and nurse congratulating me that the stork had decided to give me two gifts! The stork was a day late and two dollars short. I felt very special. I had wanted twins for my first or second pregnancy, not my fourth. The old saying says be careful what you ask for or you may just get it, and I did. According to the ultrasound, I was in my first trimester. The twins' due date was the latter part of May 1995. After that news, I dragged myself to the car and drove home in silence. My usual routine was to drive with the music on full blast. When I made it home, Bishop Abe Richardson was sitting in the living room visiting with Jeff. I shared the news and then plopped onto the sofa next to Jeff.

Bishop Richardson said, "Something told me to come check on you all."

I said, "Yes, God, please pray for us."

On January 2, 1995, I started having contractions. This time it was alarming to me since my babies were not expected to arrive until the end of May. We had our babysitter come watch the girls while Jeff took me to the hospital. Once we arrived at the hospital's emergency room, I was transported immediately to the labor and delivery wing. By this time, my contractions were 15 minutes apart. Preterm labor is dangerous and can result in premature birth. Several risk factors are possible with babies born prematurely, such as problems with their organs, long-term intellectual and developmental disabilities, and problems with their lungs.

Immediately, the doctor admitted me and placed me on bed rest. The medication terbutaline (Brethine) was administered intravenously (IV). The purpose of Brethine was to help my twins' lungs mature faster and potentially delay delivery for several days. My third day in the hospital, Dee Dee called to check on me and asked, "Why is your voice so shaky?"

I said, "I think it's the medication they gave me." I told her it's called Brethine.

At the time, Dee Dee was a pharmaceutical rep, and she looked up the purpose of the meds. Then she asked, "Are you asthmatic?"

I stated "No."

She said, "Ask if they could prescribe you another medication. You sound like you have a difficult time talking."

Besides the tremors, my heart felt like it was beating 110 beats per minute. The medication was discontinued per the doctor. Nonetheless, I remained on bed rest in the hospital and at home off and on for six to seven weeks. Sometimes I spent four-five days in the hospital then the remaining days at home. For the most part, exhaustion was an understatement for how I was feeling and the toll the pregnancy was taking on my body. I had to lie still and had an IV for roughly 28 days.

During this time, my husband was working second shift at Flex-N-Gate Corporation as a machinist. So, his sisters Karen, Shirley, and Anne alternated weeks to help care for us. My sister DD came to fill the gap for a few days because Jeff's brother, John Jr., passed away unexpectedly. Shirley, Tee, Jeff and the girls drove up to Chicago for the funeral. Karen came back with Jeff and the girls.

One particular Thursday, Jeff took the day off from work. Karen made a scrumptious dinner, and we were watching the TV show *ER*. Right when I was about to dig into my lasagna and garlic toast, all of a sudden, my water broke. It was only Thursday, February 16th. Jeff and I made it to the hospital about 9:30 p.m. I would have preferred to have a natural birth without an epidural, but the birth plan was not up to me this time. Baby number one was on top and kicking baby number two. And baby number two was in a posterior position, also known as a "sunny side up," where the baby's head was down but facing my abdomen, and the baby's skull (occipital) was against my pelvis.

The pain was unbearable, and I didn't think I was capable of going through labor ever again. All I could do was utter to myself repeatedly, "God, please help me!" A statement my mother used to say ran across my mind: "God won't put no more on you than you can handle." I wondered if God had mixed me up with someone else. Truly no disrespect was intended. However, I had nothing to give physically, mentally, and emotionally. Nausea and dry heaves took over, and I was sick to my stomach.

Then, I was being prepped for a C-section since baby number two's heart rate was falling. My preference was to be put under, but that wasn't an option as it was deemed too risky. The nurses asked if they could say the Lord's prayer while the anesthesiologist injected the epidural in my spinal cord. They didn't have to ask me twice. I was happy they were believers of Jesus Christ. Through the surgery, I continued to have dry heaves, and Jeff held the puck pail up to my mouth. Also, he assured me he was going to get a vasectomy soon after the birth of the twins. I don't know if that was going to make me feel better while I was being butchered. That was one of the most irrelevant comments I ever heard. The next thing I noticed was everybody in the operating room discussing sports, including Jeff.

The last thing I remember was the doctor saying baby one is a girl and baby two is a boy. Jelisa weighed 2 pounds and Jeffrey Jr. weighed 3 pounds. They were in the neonatal intensive care unit (NICU) for 31 days. Once I was settled in my room, sadly, Jeff went to call his brother John Jr. like he always did after our babies were born. With all the excitement, he totally forgot his brother had died the previous month.

CHAPTER VII

EXPLOSION PHASE: BLACK, BLUE, AND BROKEN

The twins had reached the terrible two stage. Lawd, the universal language, "No, no, and no!" I'm not sure how and why this is so prevalent among children of all ethnicities and nationalities. Jelisa wouldn't verbalize it as much as Jeffrey Jr., aka Jay, but she rolled her big ping-pong ball eyes and pursed her lips, which caused her deep dimples to sink deeper into her face. However, Jay's response was "No, thank you," with a tone and grin similar to a mischievous Cheshire cat. Age two was the appropriate time to introduce the infamous potty chair with a reverse child psychology twist.

"Hey Jay, you are becoming a big boy, and big boys don't wear Pampers. Would you like to go with Mommy to pick out some Spiderman underoos underwear sets?"

"No, thank you, just buy me the T-shirt."

My face mirrored Jelisa without the big eyes and deep dimples. On the flip side, Jelisa was excited to pick out her Wonder Woman underoos and welcomed potty training like a champ. By spring break, Jelisa was sporting her underoos like she was walking down a Victoria Secret runway. Nevertheless, Jay spent spring and most of the summer with the potty chair and his underoos T-shirt.

They attended the Washington Early Childhood Education part-time like their older sisters. Then I decided I needed to go to work part-time since everyone was in school. A part time/temporary job would help build the family budget and my resume. A temporary employment agency assigned me to work at Carle Arbours, a retirement facility, as a dietary aide about 20 hours a week from 4 p.m.-8 p.m. The hours were convenient considering Jeff's work schedule was 5:30 a.m.-1 p.m.

During the day, I had time to get the kids off to school, clean the house, prepare dinner, get the twins off the bus, and volunteer at Prairie Elementary School a couple of days of the week, all before going to work. Before long, I was offered a full-time position with a phenomenal schedule from 6 a.m.-2:30 p.m. Sadly, Jeff didn't appear to be happy with my afforded opportunity. As I knew the full-time hours would help with our budget and we needed additional health insurance, I recall going to the restroom after completing new hire paperwork with a human resources assistant.

With a sense of disappointment and tears rolling down my face, I was thinking, "You should be much further along than this." Frankly, I didn't view myself as better than my dietary colleagues. I just wanted better options for me and my children, and $6.85 an hour wasn't going to get us there. Apart from that, everything was falling into place. My friend Jenella and her sister

Jenique were babysitting all five of our children and made sure they made it to and from school. Additionally, our children and I were so blessed because they would take my children to their church on Sundays when I had to work.

Every morning when I rose at 4:45 a.m., it was dark as midnight no matter the season. As usual, I blasted the stereo to officially start my day with *The Preacher's Wife* soundtrack or the Great Women of Gospel CD and one of my favorites, Sandra Crouch's "You Abide in Me." The sound of gospel music in the wee hours of the morning was the alarm clock for my children. There was only one bathroom and seven people, so preparation the night before made the a.m. routine quite smooth. We ate dinner from 6 p.m.-6:45p.m., had bath time 7 p.m.-8 p.m., and bedtime was 8:30 p.m., including for me. I loaded the kids into the car to drive one block away to Jenella's house by 5:35 a.m. Then, I was off to Windsor Road to make it to Savoy, IL, for my 6 a.m. shift. Champaign-Urbana is such a small town that commute time was literally 10-12 minutes at the most.

Arrival through the back door to the kitchen was always met with soul music, chatter, and the smell of bacon, eggs, and oatmeal, and a "Hey, Girl" from my colleagues. Some of the other coworkers' greetings were "Good morning, Adrienne." My bushy-tailed and wide-eyed responses were, "Hey, y'all" and "Good morning to you." One member of this esteemed bunch was the head cook, who prepared all the meals like a black culinary chef from the southern region of America. Her gravy was never lumpy or oversaturated with the bland taste of white flour. The smoothness of the gravy was comparable to Gold Bond Ultimate Diabetics' Dry Skin Relief Hydrating Lotion. My palette had encountered so many lumps from so-called homemade gravy, some flour was stuck on the roof of my mouth. Geez, Louise! It was a celebratory moment when the cook and I were introduced for the second time in the kitchen. The first time we met was under sobering circumstances. Her granddaughter's incubator was right next to Jay's and kitty-corner from Jelisa's in the NICU. Our babies were thriving and acting their age, saying "No," which was rewarding seeing how once upon a time they were unable to nurse and breathe on their own.

This assisted living facility was a nice place. It was clean, the food was good, and the staff worked together to provide warm and stellar services. Nevertheless, the certified nursing assistants (CNA) had an enormous workload compared to the licensed practicing nurse (LPN) and registered nurse (RN). The CNAs were fully responsible for approximately 20-25 patients' hygiene, serving their meals, and any and everything needed in between. Some days, the dietary staff and housekeeping staff would assist the CNAs with feeding residents who were less mobile. We would also empty waste baskets in their rooms. We were not trained to fulfill some of the duties, but the CNAs' staff had a high attrition rate, and the LPN and RN congregated at the nurse's station quite often, unless dispensing medication.

On the other hand, the kitchen was always lit with interesting urban conversation about black sports figures, the *Essence* magazine cover that Dwayne Wayne and Whitley Gilbert from the sitcom *A Different World* graced, and the popular movie *Booty Call* with the funny-ass cast, Jamie Foxx, Vivica Fox, Tamala Jones, and Tommy Davidson. Ironically, the father of pudding pops Bill Cosby publicly slammed the movie and accused the plot of "sending the wrong message about sex." Now, looking back, the "pot calling the kettle black" was on full display.

One of my favorites was singing and talking to my colleagues about the latest R&B and hip-hop hits, such as Keith Sweat's "Twisted" and "Hail Mary" by Tupac. Days when I needed to be alone and ponder, I would wear my headphones and work the dish machine while listening to my eclectic taste in music. For instance, music by Rev. Timothy Wright, "Master Can You Use Me," "My Philosophy," Boogie Down Productions (BDP), and one of my old-time favorites by Crystal Gayle, "Don't It Make My Brown Eyes Blue." Overall, I enjoyed the experience and the numerous people I was able to work with and build relationships with.

Springtime was approaching with the excitement of daylight-saving time. Sunrise at 5 a.m., birds singing, and bumble bees buzzing around from one flower to the next. The warmth of the sun shining through the Venetian blinds was like "God bless the sun to grace my cheek" by John O'Donohue per Rev. Dr. Moss. During this season, the Jehovah's Witnesses and Latter-Day Saints, aka Mormons, would go from door to door and evangelize. I would enter into a conversation with them because growing up in Chicago, if they knocked on the door and/or rang the doorbell my parents would make us stop in our tracks and be quiet with the hopes of them leaving. At times, they were quite persistent; it felt like they would stand on the front porch for at least 10 minutes while we were at a standstill in the living room. Their presence bears a resemblance to the scene from the movie *Friday*, when the character Aunt Esther from the television show *Sanford and Son* was a Jehovah's Witness and banged consistently on Craig's front door like she was the police. Consequently, Craig answered with a "What and no, thank you." Aunt Esther's infamous response was, "You half dead motherfucker." Unlike Craig, my parents didn't answer the knock and wouldn't have greeted God's people in that manner.

During the course of my life, I had become curious about other Christian sects. So, I would engage in discussion with the missionaries. In particular, two young ladies from Latter Day Saints Church greeted me while I was watering the grass. That was the start of a long-standing discussion on doctrine. My only familiarity with the Mormon church was the commercials on television. Also, they heavily populated the state of Utah. However, it was enriching and enlightening to learn about Joseph Smith, the prophet, who saw God and Jesus in his first vision. Subsequently, the visits started veering into talks about life, travel, and future goals. Interestingly, the young ladies' missionary trip had come to an end. Surprisingly, they shared my name with incoming missionaries, and I welcomed the discussions on two different Christian religions.

At the same time, the Jehovah's Witnesses would walk up and down our street to evangelize that there is only one God, and that's Jehovah not the Holy Trinity of God's presence, God as the father, as the Son (Jesus Christ), and as the Holy Spirit. One particular day, my front door was open, and a lady accompanied by a man knocked on the screen door. Introductions were made, and the interreligious dialogue began. It appeared our curiosity was aroused.

They asked, "Can we come back Saturday and share more literature that can answer some of the questions you have raised?"

"Absolutely. See y'all Saturday."

Saturday came back around; the couple came back as they had stated. Our neighbor Tim was visiting with Jeff when the couple arrived. Once again, introductions were made, and we came to find out Tim and the gentlemen were former colleagues. It made for some pleasantries but lacked the interest of the previous conversations.

Acute Victim

One particular day, I was at work and received a call from Jeff. He said, "What is this? I hear that you have people coming into my house."

"What are you talking about? I am working and busy." Click. I hung the phone up.

Jeff had great difficulty with trust. What I realized was people who struggle with trusting are usually the most untrustworthy. Jeff always behaved as if someone was out to get him or scam him in some form or fashion. But in actuality, he was a scammer.

Soon after I entered the front door, I went to the bedroom to get out of my work clothes and take a shower. Before I could remove my clothes, here comes Jeff saying, "The kids told me some guy was in the house."

"I don't have time to deal with another man, especially while trying to deal with you!" A frown and a huff and puff came from him.

He raised his voice: "You bitch! You think you all that!"

Retaliation for me was to not entertain his rage. An exhausting feeling overcame me. He had the complexity of Dr. Jekyll and Mr. Hyde. One minute it seemed he was okay, but then an alter ego would appear to defend his honor. Sadly, he dishonored himself, yet he blamed everyone else. I released a fatigued exhale. "The cure for your exhaustion is intimacy with Jesus," (Priscilla Shirer, You're Right Where You Need to Be). Then, he pushed me, and I pushed him back.

"Don't ever touch me again," I uttered.

He pushed me again. Rain was in the forecast that day, so I had taken an umbrella to work. The umbrella was still in my hand when I went to my bedroom.

"I'm not bullshitting. Keep your hands off me."

That's the playground rule: Keep your hands to yourself. He hit me, and the umbrella landed on his head and face several times.

Then, out of nowhere, he swung, and the next thing I knew I was on the floor. I was so dizzy I couldn't get up. There was blood coming from everywhere: my forehead, my nose, and I was coughing up blood. My work uniform was soaked in blood, and my work shoes were no longer white. By then, he was apologetic and trying to help me up off the carpet.

"STOP, STOP! Take my kids to Brenda's house so they won't see me like this."

Brenda was my neighbor who lived two houses down from me, and her daughter, Christy, babysat our children frequently. As crazy as it sounds, I had him drive me to Carle Hospital Emergency Room because I was still dizzy and didn't want to bring any attention to my house. The unfortunate part about my decision was that my shame superseded my safety and his accountability. Historically, the black community hasn't had the best experience with the intent behind the slogan "protect and serve," especially black women victimized by domestic violence. I didn't realize my choice to hoard my abuse was a historic practice among black women and that I was helping contribute to the old practice of protecting black men who abuse.[7]

The registrar at the front desk took me to triage at once. The triage nurse asked, "What happened?" She was sympathetic. "Who did it?"

"My husband did it."

"Where is he?" she asked.

"I'm not sure."

The Urbana Police arrested Jeff as he was leaving the ER. The ER staff put me in an examining room for hours. Honestly, I don't recall being examined by any doctors. I slept for several hours before the nurse asked if I had anyone to call. I don't remember calling anyone. Apparently, I call DeeDee. My mother and two sisters, DeeDee and Nicky, drove down to Urbana from Chicago to pick me up from the hospital late that night. Their faces were struck with horror, fright, and dismay when they entered my examination room. I figured my face was in bad shape, but I wasn't able to see it since it was covered with all the blood from earlier that day. Also, I still had my work clothes on, and I had to wear my work shoes home with gobs of blood.

The attentive nurse provided me with my discharge papers and explained my diagnosis. You have a broken nose, a black eye, and five stitches above your left eyebrow. You have an appointment with the Maxillofacial surgery department in two weeks after the swelling goes down. Basically, my face was disfigured, and my children saw it when we picked them up from Brenda's house. This was the explosive phase, where I was black, blue, and broken.

Once Jeff made bail, he went back to Chicago to live with one of his sisters. Luckily, I became full-time and earned a great deal of personal time off (PTO). Graciously, Willa, the director of food service, granted me additional time off with pay. It took roughly two weeks for the swelling of my nose and my left eye to go down. During the time of healing, Mrs. Maryanne, a church member, stopped by the house to check on me. She shared that growing up in the church in the South, divorce was frowned upon. According to Mrs. Maryanne, she embodied that religious doctrine.

Subsequently, while staring at me in dismay and with sympathy, she said, "I believe God doesn't want any of his children to be mistreated, especially if they are married." Then she embraced me tightly. "God loves you," she cried.

One of the nicest people I know, also came to visit me. She explained, "A couple of times, I was headed to your house, and Jeff told me, 'My wife is busy and she isn't able to go walking with you today.'"

Unbeknownst to me, Jeff had implemented isolation tactics by trying to control who I could see and talk to and where I could go.

Jenella said, "I should've known something wasn't right".

"It's okay. You can't take responsibility for a grown-ass man," I sympathized.

It was time to go back to work, and I was ready to get a plan of action in motion. Well, by this time Jenella and Jenique could no longer babysit. The twins had to stay in Chicago with Jeff until a new childcare arrangement was made. His mother and sister helped care for the twins while Jeff was at work during the evening. It was devastating for my girls to reside with me in Urbana with the twins living in Chicago. My weekends off, the girls and I would hit I-57 north to visit Jelisa and Jay. This living arrangement lasted for the longest few months of my life. Most importantly, the thought of others having influence on my children during their zero to five stage of life was quite worrisome. This unsettling feeling caused me to make another regrettable choice to let Jeff move back after all the hell he had brought about.

Guilt and Shame

It's amazing how desperation, shame, guilt, and economic uncertainties can be influential. Ironically, I was concerned about my twins being influenced, but I was influenced by despair and my lower socioeconomic status (SES). According to the Institute for Family Studies, one of the eight reasons women stay in abusive relationships is due to financial constraints, such as "the abuser limits the current or future earning potential of the victim as a strategy of power and control," and 94-99% of victims/survivors have also experienced economic abuse.[8] From the time I first knew Jeff, he had a difficult time personifying self-discipline. Prime examples were not being able to complete basic training in the United States Army and not possessing a consistent work history from 1992-2003. But he easily adapted to a kind of carelessness with rash behaviors—case in point, exposing our children to domestic violence (DV).

CHAPTER VIII

"A MAN HAS ALWAYS WANTED TO LAY ME DOWN BUT HE NEVER WANTED TO PICK ME UP" – EARTHA KITT

It was rare for the kids to see us fighting; however, they probably heard us raising our voices sometimes. It was the elephant in the room, and I imagined it was an indescribable feeling for them. I prayed for divine guidance to fix it. I noticed a change in my children's temperaments. They weren't as bubbly and sociable but more cautious and quiet. In addition, my son was diagnosed with anxiety at five years old. Instantaneously, I knew I needed to show my kids I cared, was the stable parent, and was their protector from the trauma of domestic violence.

Over the years, I enrolled children in numerous activities—a cheerleading program, taekwondo, band, a "Brothers and Sistas" program at Prairie School, Urbana Park District basketball and summer camp, Arts Camp, Girls Engage in Mathematics Engineering and Science (GAMES) Camp, Principal's Scholars program, Swimming lessons and Urbana Swim Team, Computer Science Camp, AAU Basketball, regional travel softball team, Urbana School District girls basketball team, girls soccer team, boys football team and wrestling team, traveling wrestling team, football, cheer squad and Upward Bound College Preparatory Program, and College for Kids. Over and above, the most important social supports that helped were the youth ministries at Dublin Street Church of Christ located in Urbana, IL, and First Christian Church in Champaign, IL. I'm sharing all of this because this was the trajectory to guide the spiritual beliefs that give meaning to life, self-esteem, and self-efficacy for my children that God blessed me with. It wasn't until 2007 that I learned the meaning of "Protective Factors" from The National Child Traumatic Stress Network (NCTSN) when I became a Home Visitor and a Teen Parent Group Coordinator for the Early Childhood Mental Health Department, formerly known as Champaign County Mental Health Center (CCMHC).

I thank God for the spiritual insight and guidance. Children of domestic violence experiences and responses can be quite different depending on their temperament, as previously mentioned, and the child's proximity to the violence, for example, the severity of the violence, the children's age, and the quality of the children's relationships with both parents.

One of the most dispiriting things I witnessed over time was the shift in all five of my kids' personalities due to domestic violence. Was it possible for them to regain who nature intended them to become, I wondered.[9] From the beginning to the present,

I try to let my four daughters and one son know I see them and love them from the crown of their heads to the soles of their feet. I found it hard to nurture their many strengths without acknowledging their passion and potential. I think they knew I was their cheering squad and biggest fan. Despite being the loudest in the stands specifically for them, my encouragement was sometimes viewed as an assertive nudge or a psychological tactic. That was perfectly fine with me since it was all attributed to a mother's love without any harm intended.

In contrast, my husband enjoyed playing psychological games as well as chess. The aroma of baked barbecued pork chops, homemade potato salad, smothered cabbage & turnip greens with turkey thigh, and homemade cornbread with a half cup of Jiffy mix flowed throughout the house. Here comes Jeff, who is arriving home with a couple of colleagues. Without fail, I prepared extra food out of habit and offered his guests some dinner. I had seen them several times at the bank where I worked, since they cashed their payroll checks there. When they came into my home, they looked at me and said to him, "That's your wife?"

"Yeah", he said.

They chuckled. "What does she want with you," they blurred.

After they left, things turned a little dark. Jeff was angry and said to me, "Do you know them?"

"Not really. I've seen them at the bank a few times."

"It seems like they really know you."

"You're the one who brought them into our home," I exclaimed.

"Have you been with any of them?"

"No. Don't start that shit with me!"

Similar questions, outbursts, and accusations would become more frequent as time went on. Gradually, Jeff started with the insults and trying to belittle me. He would manipulate the situation to make it appear as if I was putting him down with my work and school achievements. "As a psychological abuser, he constantly tried to undermine my sense of self-worth and confidence". My most effective response was no verbal response, just a look and a nod! When he realized I'd had enough, he came back and apologized.[10] I was burned out with his apologies a long time before. Cognitively, I screamed, "Why, why, why did I allow him to come back? He's more work than five children, a menstrual cycle, and a 10-page research paper."

"I didn't mean it like that, and I think you're bright. I don't want you to wear yourself out with your busy schedule, working full-time, going to school part-time, and volunteering at the kids' schools," he insincerely sympathized. It was clear to me that my husband wanted authentic and unwavering intimacy while he betrayed me with false intimacy.

In the report of Safe Lives Ending Domestic Abuse, 90% of practitioners agreed that psychological violence is usually interspersed with warmth and kindness to create emotional confusion.[11]

It's hard to recognize the early stages of abuse because it's murky. It's not abusive throughout the entire relationship. I came to understand abuse during the escalation phase, but the clues were in the early parts of our relationship. His self-abuse and implied accusations were all signs leading to harm. Looking back, I realize that in the beginning abuse had such subtlety to it. Abruptness was poised as gentle satire. The cycle of violence starts with words that you could easily fail to notice. "The burden of proof tends to fall on victims/survivors that endured psychological violence."[12]

I paid heed to Jeff's recurring addictive behaviors, such as missing work several days in a row, no money, abusiveness, increased alcohol intake to defer the craving for crack-cocaine, bloodshot eyes, short temper, and walking in and out the house all times of the night. Obviously, he wasn't in his right state of mind and tried gaslighting me frequently. This was way before gaslighting was a term, but it's a notable practice among abusers. He had the unmitigated gall to accuse me of sneaking someone in the back door entrance through the backyard and claimed he saw it all while visiting one of his drug buddies in the apartment complex behind the house. Fed up was an understatement for how I felt about this psychological war with the relapsed addict. Jeff liked to play mind games to strategize his next act of terror and denigrate prior to physical abuse.[13]

At first, the mental tug-a-war was taxing. Next, I recalled being in the fifth grade. I had a fight with a boy in the sixth grade because he said I tripped him during a gym tournament of kick baseball when he was running around the bases. Actually, that little punk had no speed. He was running around the bases like someone who didn't know how to play the game. So, he told me after he got his punk ass up off the floor the infamous "2:30 p.m!" This meant we're fighting when school dismisses at 2:30 p.m. Two of the top strategies for when black girls would fight was to put Vaseline on your face to help avoid scratches and remove earrings so they can't snatch them out of your ear lobes. I figured he was going to get outside and try to showboat with a boxing stance like he was a student of Larry Holmes, former WBC Heavyweight Champion from 1978 to 1983. The bell rang, and everyone was running down the stairs from the third floor. He started walking toward me like he was big and bad. Too bad he didn't approach those bases in the same manner. I kindly took off my shoe and committed to beat him with the heel of it like the winner of the kick baseball tournament. During all the ass-kicking, I did catch a right blow beneath my right eye. My bobs and weaves weren't up to speed. Damn!

So that evening, I was riding in the car with my parents, and Daddy was like, "What happened to your eye?"

I said, "I had a fight with this boy."

My Daddy's response was, "Did you win?

I said, "Yes."

He said, "Okay!"

That experience in my life reminded me that when I no longer was able to physically defend myself from my husband, I had to depend on my psychological defense. One day he came home and asked if we had eaten dinner yet.

"The kids and I already ate, but your dinner is on the stove," I replied

Jeff looked at me then the stove then a box of rat poison on the kitchen counter right next to the stove. I proceeded to tell him I thought I saw a mouse in the house. That particular night, his appetite escaped him. In the back of my mind I said, "Yes, Daddy, I won!"

Two significant incidents catalyzed Jeff's move out of the house and the marriage. Meanwhile, he was in-between jobs for the 40th time. I was still working full-time and was a part-time student at Parkland Community College majoring in accounting. The evening of my final exam, Jeff was nowhere to be found. Class started promptly at 6 p.m. I didn't arrive at class until 6:45 p.m. Luckily, Brenda came to my rescue and watched the kids at the very last minute. When I arrived home at 8:30 p.m., there was still no Jeff. As always, I was appreciative of Brenda and her family's support. I extended an apology to Brenda.

She said, "There is no need. How do you think you did on your exam?"

"Good," I replied.

Jeff casually walked into the room at about 10:30 p.m. His excuse was, "I was busy."

"Did you get a new job, or do you have discharge papers from the Emergency Room?" I asked.

"You always have something smart to say."

"No, I'm not a smart aleck, I'm addressing an important matter like an adult," I yelled! "You're trying to sabotage my collegiate studies by not coming home on time to watch our children. It's okay. I blame myself for allowing myself to remain in this madness for so long. First time, shame on you. Second, shame on me. I distinctly recall when you said you're too good for me and my dumb ass said no, we'll be fine. You are showing me more and more why you say what you say. Dr. Maya Angelou said it best: 'When someone shows you who they are, believe them the first time."

"But He Never Wanted to Pick Me Up"

He took that statement as an invitation and hauled off and slapped me. I returned the favor. We looked like the scene from the movie *Monster In-Law* with Jane Fonda and Jennifer Lopez when they slapped each other repeatedly five times in the course of one minute on the day of the wedding. Beyond belief, he spat in my face and told me he had a gun in the closet and was going to kill me if I hit him again or said anything. He sat on the bed and mean-mugged me while I sat in the chair. I refused to sleep in the bed or fall asleep while he was awake. I was so anxious, I couldn't sleep, which is totally unlike me. I have always gone to bed between 8:30 p.m. and 9 p.m. since elementary school. I drifted off to sleep about 3 a.m. until 3:45 a.m. My mind was racing a mile a minute. I started to reflect on the years of Jeff not stepping up to the plate as a man, husband, and father. I didn't trap him into our relationship nor marriage by having children. At that very moment, I felt disappointed that he reneged on our marriage and fatherhood—his parental duties more than anything.

Neither of us were accustomed to seeing fathers not take care of their children, especially not our fathers. He didn't have the emotional capacity or discipline to be a provider or a team player. He exuded his energy in the pleasantries of laying down my body, interacting with my mind, and having access to my soul. However, he didn't have the same drive to uplift me personally, professionally, and with my spiritual endeavors. The scripture that came to mind was 1 Corinthians 13:11, *"When I was a child, I spoke as a child, I understood as a child, I thought as a child: but when I became a man, I put away childish things"* (NKJV). Unfortunately, Jeff never put away childish things.

So, the next morning, before I went off to my full-time job, I had to reintroduce Jeffrey Spires, Sr. to the former Adrienne "Paddy" Young. The kids were off to school. I pulled the large stockpot from under the kitchen cabinet and filled it with hot water. It was on the burner for approximately 10 minutes. The H2O was scorching hot, and the steam filled the kitchen. Cautiously, I removed the pot with two oven mitts and slowly walked down the hall to our bedroom, where Jeff was asleep as if he had an actual job and had worked a double shift. I placed the stockpot onto the dresser, carefully. Then, I removed the oven mitts and sat them next to the pot where I stood.

I said, "Jeff. Jeff, wake up."

He did a halfway stretch and opened one eye then the other. "Hey, what's going on?" he asked.

"You see this big-ass pot of boiling water? I contemplated, God knows I contemplated, if I should or shouldn't drench you with it. Mainly, I just wanted to show you Paddy," I said.

A peculiar look gradually came across his face. Our eyes interlocked, accompanied by an intense stare. Not one word was spoken. I turned around and walked down the corridor while looking out my peripheral view. Off to work Paddy went.

After the morning's interaction between Jeff and I, he started looking through his peripheral view figuratively and literally. My demeanor went from nice to passive aggressive. For example, he came home very late one night and apologized.

My response, "It's okay. Are you hungry?" followed up with an erotic forehead kiss. The next time, I put the security chain on the door so he would have to knock on the door to enter the house.

I believe the last straw for him was when he woke up the next morning with torticollis, basically a twisted neck or wryneck.

"Pat, I can't move my damn neck," he whimpered.

"What happened?" I questioned. "Do you need some ice or icy hot?"

"When I went to sleep last night, my neck was okay. What the hell?"

"Maybe when you fell asleep, you adjusted your head in a crooked way."

That afternoon, Jeff went to the hospital and returned with a neck brace and the official diagnosis of torticollis. He came into the kitchen and looked at me with so much contempt.

"You know you did something to me in the middle of the night," Jeff claimed.

"Pardon me? I wouldn't do such a thing to you in your sleep," I said in a suspicious whisper. "Now, you know me, I would let you see me coming and not sneak around like a thief in the night."

The aura of silence entered the room for a slight moment. Then, I casually strolled to the living room to complete my application to Eastern Illinois University.

CHAPTER IX

THE UNBEARABLE ESCALATION

Separate to Live

So, here comes Jeff, rehashing the wryneck again. "I know damn well you did something to me while I was asleep."

"As I stated before, I was not trying to harm you while you were asleep. I can't speak for what happened to you during the time you were sleeping because I was in a comatose state. As you know, I have always gone to bed early, so I don't have any idea what you are referring to."

The next day Jeff decided to tell me that he didn't want to live anymore if I wasn't able to love him, treat him and/or support him as a man.

He said, "You are supposed to be my best friend."

I muttered, "Negro, what!"

The Unbearable Escalation

The imaginary bubbles with words appeared in the air with the following quotes from him: "You think you are better than me" and "You need to be the wife you professed you would be during your wedding vows." I could have sworn I heard a violin playing in the background while he was trying to play on my emotions with his coercion and threatening tactics. This is another spoke in the "power and control" wheel.

"Jeff, I am the wife that you wanted and more than you ever anticipated. I am a lady in public and your wildest fantasy at night. I cook like a southern chef. I encourage you like I am your counselor and/or mentor. Also, you don't know how to define a friend. On the other hand, you don't do the same for me in return. Sexually, you're arousing. However, you don't reciprocate by uplifting me when I'm in need of encouragement as a young mother and wife. I have no immediate family in this town you suggested we relocate to. I'm loving you and our children with all I have to offer. I'm trying to make it better for the whole family. My hard work is for the family at large. Not for me only. I don't have any addictions. Yes, there are times there are mental concerns because I'm exhausted and embody Monday blues, but I don't cause any damage or harm to our family."

Then he reiterated, "You think you are better than me."

"You ignoramus! I never thought I was better than you. You need to think more highly of yourself. I was under the impression we were a team because we have so much to live for and potential in this world. Okay, let's put the potential to work. Let's stop feeling sorry for ourselves. You played organized baseball in high school, right? It takes discipline to be on any team and support your teammates. I too am a team player, and it takes discipline for me to accomplish the goals I set before me. So, lets fucking do it! Let's just do it! I'm exhausted mentally and physically. Is there anything else we need to talk about? Is there anything else we need to cover?" I said, with irritation.

After that mess, I made my way back to the living room to sit on the couch and watch some music videos on BET.

Later that evening, Jeff was in the bedroom and decided to try to take his own life by taking a bunch of pills with an alcoholic drink. I can't recall the drink, but there was an empty liquor bottle on the floor near the bed. Thank God, the children were in bed. I made sure my kids stayed on a bedtime schedule. I threw cold water on his face and shook him vigorously until he responded with slurring speech. We walked to the bathroom, which was right next to our bedroom, so he could get in the shower under more cold water. Slowly, his speech became audible and he was able to enunciate his words. I was able to hear and understand Jeff while he was under the influence of pills and alcohol.

"Pat, just let me die."

"I don't have time for you to die on me," I spoke. "So, you want to die in the house with your wife and five children? Negro, please! What is it you need help with?"

Honestly, in the middle of my mind, I was thinking he doesn't have what it takes to survive in this world. He doesn't have what it takes to survive in this household, and I was his source of support in Urbana. In addition, he had another support system in Chicago that consisted of his mother and sisters. The next morning, I called one of his sisters and told her what had taken place the previous night. They came down to visit for that weekend to provide him with moral support. Usually, they would arrive on a Friday evening and check into the hotel and stay until Saturday evening, but this particular time their visit lasted until Sunday evening. Per usual, we spent some quality time together, such as hanging out at the house, cooking dinner, chatting, and watching movies. His mother and sister conversed with him and shared encouraging words along with some Bible verses.

The following day, I informed Jeff he needed to leave again and please don't return.

He was reluctant and a little irate. "Why? Why!"

"You have to go because once again you're not concerned about your life, which you have shown me numerous times. You have tried to take my life. You have exposed our children to violence. You need to go."

He didn't like the sound of my demand. Once more he had to express his disapproval with ridicule and a violent outburst.

"You raggedy bitch, I don't need to stay here anyway! There are plenty of other women who would love for me to live with them," he screamed. (In the back of my mind: Please don't disappoint them.)

He headed out the front door as I was shutting it behind him. Immediately, he did an about face and aggressively pushed his way back into the living room.

"Please go," I urged.

This was identical to the scene from *Waiting to Exhale* when a drunk Troy showed up two hours late to Robin's condo to go meet his family. Robin kindly said, "I don't like this," and Troy said, "Why not?" Troy's flaws were on full display, but he boasted about his self-perception of being a great catch. "As soon as a man or brother show you genuine interest, you bitches act simple. Then you wonder why we go out with white women." Before he left per Robin's request, Troy had the audacity to throw an orange at her balcony with the hopes of hitting her. Good thing he missed, and Robin picked up the orange and hit him, presumably in the back of his head. "Augh!" Troy groaned.

"What if I don't?" Jeff replied. "What you gonna do? Whip my ass? Or better yet poison my food or be a coward and try to kill me in my sleep?" he yelled.

The whole time, I listened attentively with a defensive posture and the thought of how I would defend myself.

"I don't want to stay in this motherfucker anyway!"

As long as I have known Jeff, he has never really exhibited healthy coping skills. Before he left, he reached his hand way back and balled his fist, then punched a gigantic hole in the wall near the front door. Next, he exited, and I instantly attached the security chain on the front door.

His violent ass kicked in the door and said, "Bye."

The door became dislodged and was swinging from the hinges. After his tantrum, he left. Thankfully, he was finally gone. A few days later, the kids and I were getting in the car to go to pick up a family pleaser pizza from Monical's Pizza and salad with the famous sweet & tart French salad dressing. The night was brightened with flaring stars and the peaking moon right before it became a full moon. I started the car and inserted my "House" music CD and proceeded to blast it before exiting the driveway.

The Unbearable Escalation

Out of nowhere, Jeff jumped on top of the hood of the car telling me, "Stop, Stop!"

The kids were shocked and frightened at the unexpected ordeal. "Mama, mama," they screamed.

Now, it ran across my mind to gun the accelerator then slam on the brakes so he would fall in the middle of the street so we could go pick up the Family Pleaser and my favorite French dressing. I was hangry and tired. Once again, I didn't want to have the police in our business. Nor did I want to give the neighbors something to talk about. More often than not, Jeff was perfectly fine with showing his ass as if it was a rite of passage of manhood.

He often stated, "I'm a real nigga."

"For heaven sakes, can you please get off the hood of my car. My babies and I are hungry and need to go pick up dinner."

The entire scenario was unbearable to have to take part in. He lay, stretched, and lounged on the car hood for approximately 15 minutes, and my children had to be eyewitnesses to his deranged behavior, once again. As luck would have it, the sky was as dark as midnight. So my prayers were answered that my neighbors didn't witness anything. I sat patiently while the kids fell asleep in the car until he walked home to his new white girlfriend/roommate.

A sigh of relief came upon me. The kids and I dragged ourselves into the house without dinner and moseyed our way into bed. The next morning, we slept until about 8:30 a.m., which was considered sleeping in for us. Usually, we rose between 5 and 6 a.m. For the first time in a long time, I felt fresh, renewed, and rested. The direct opposite of the latter years of waking up next to Jeff.

Exhale

Is it so much to ask
My voice and thoughts cause your anger
My silence is a great offense
What is it you seek of me?
Tell me so I may stop your ire.

You play the wounded animal
You act the injured party
I wish nothing more than to be the spectator of this farce you show

You are a wolf that injures lambs
And yet you act as if you are but a dove
I ask that you stop and remove false white feathers
And to be true to those you fooled

I know it's but a hopeless wish
That truth and justice will prevail
I know that it's only a childish dream
For a happily ever after to exist

I now know that never will you admit to your flaws and lies
That you are in a never ending tale
Where you are an injured flower
Broken by the thorns of an ancient rose

I now see that never will your voice soften
Instead you will louden it so all may hear
You fill me with guilt I know I mustn't feel

The Unbearable Escalation

But feel it I did regardless
You make me feel responsible for things I should know I can't control
And such feelings I wish it never exists

Yet is it so much to ask
That we play as if we're porcelain this one time?
I am no longer asking you to shed your white feathers and bare your fangs
I am no longer asking you to shout your faults to the gods of the sky and earth
I now only ask that we have peace for but a moment that I may be given time to breathe

So tell me, why this request is such a chore for you
Tell me why my desire for peace is an insult to this pride you hold so dear
For everyday in my heart and soul
Amidst all your hateful words and lies
I am left with nothing more than the madness of this life

I seek solace from the storm of emotions and voices in my mind
I ask for shelter from the harsh winds and the searing heat
I ask for a simple embrace to bid away my fears
Tell me why all I get are these bitter tears

Tell it to me now so that I'd understand
Tell it to me so I may stop
If comfort in an embrace of rope is all I need
Tell it to me, so I may at last go to sleep

The Unbearable Escalation

The poem "Is it so much to ask" is an emotional abuse poem that is so descriptive of my premarital experience and marriage with Jeff. As if the author Rie Guzman was writing it with me in mind.[14] Obviously, this poem spoke not just to me and many other people. As of 2018, this powerful poem had 8.8k views. The stanza, "If comfort in an embrace of rope is all I need, Tell it to me, so I may at last go to sleep" was a figurative thought as I never contemplated suicide. My spirit and soul were restless due to the emotional bondage and domestic violence caused by Jeff's narcissism. An official separation a slippery banana peel away from a divorce helped me to "believe in the possibility to heal"[15] and grow exponentially.

As a full-time personal banker, I continued my studies at Parkland College part-time for about two to three semesters. At the same time, I would have some of the most profound conversations with the regular customers and colleagues. For instance, Mrs. Anna would talk about the importance of prayer and how she was going to start a group and invite me. One day, she told me, "You are going to write a book."

"Who me?" I said, surprised. "Girl, that would be a nap session. My life is a boring routine. However, thanks for the encouragement and inspiration."

Frequently, I waited on a customer who was a U.S. Army veteran who encouraged me to transfer to Eastern Illinois University (EIU). "You could earn credit hours with years of experience at this bank through the portfolio program. It will be perfect," he stated. Overall, there were also many great discussions with my various coworkers. The most profound of them all was my favorite colleague/friend, Besty Wilcher. We talked about family, life, marriage, and education. Besty would wait on customers and close home equity and secure loans on my behalf so I could complete homework assignments and/or get to class a little early. In addition, Besty had the biggest ear and warmest smile that my overwhelmed heart appreciated to the second power. The year 2001 was a year of "restless ambition."[16] I was eager for a dramatic change in every aspect of my life: medical, family, personal, professional, and spiritual.

Happily Divorced

The morning of September 14, 2001, I was as excited and giddy as a kid on Christmas morning with great anticipation of new gifts. I recall walking into the courtroom to finalize my divorce. I officially was on the trajectory to become a domestic violence survivor from a victim. I was on the path to pulling all the pieces of myself back together. However, that was challenging because Jeff put in the work to break me psychologically/emotionally, sexually, physically, and economically from 1993-2001. It was time to put on my positivity hat and remove negativity from my psyche.

A plan of action was devised to get my life back on track. I was in desperate need of a new start after that marriage. First, I started walking every morning before work and some evenings. Second, I began counseling sessions and then stopped going after the fourth session. The sessions focused more on the amazement of my resiliency and articulation. Oddly, after the second visit, I started leading the sessions. It wasn't until four years later that I found the ultimate therapist. Third, I started my undergraduate studies full-time to reinvent myself and become more marketable.

Fourth, I developed strategies to stay focused and reach my family, personal, and spiritual goals. Fifth, I embraced the various circles of support from family, friends, and my church family. Finally, my sister DD's unwavering support and love helped me to feel reborn again, like the "circle of life," "Thus, when humans die, they are not dead but merely reborn to begin another circle of life." Yes, I referenced a song from the movie *Lion King*. She was the comfort I needed while in the lion's den.

Rebuilt & Repositioned Family: Dublin Street Church of Christ

This was the time when I was repositioning and rebuilding my family. For me and my children, it was a very gratifying and momentous time. We had the perfect opportunity to set up our spiritual journey at this point in time.

We were invited to attend the anniversary dinner of my friend Marion's church, Dublin Street Church of Christ. An endearing evening of gospel hymns, warm conversation, and a savory menu of fried chicken, fish, potatoes with gravy and onions, ice cold sweet tea, chocolate cake, and apple pie a la mode rounded out the evening.

We became members of Dublin Street Church soon after, where Pastor Jackson was the senior pastor. My children and I thoroughly enjoyed the youth ministry, Bible study, and worship service. The youth ministry was led by Brother McElrath and the late Sister Bradley, who facilitated Bible study, Sunday School, and took the youth to events and the National Youth Conferences of

Church and Christ. The youth ministry at Dublin Street combined the rigor of summer school with the joy of summer camp.

The youth ministries took the children to NBA Indiana Pacers games, Six Flags, and youth conferences in Wisconsin. My kids packed their own bags the second time they attended the conference because they were old enough and had traveled out of Illinois on more than one occasion. I also bought new underwear for my children whenever we went out of town, a habit I learned from my mother. On this occasion, I asked Jay several times if he had packed everything on the list. "Yes, Mama," he replied with an exhausted sigh. After they returned home, his sisters couldn't wait to tell me the youth minister had gone to Walmart to buy Jay's underwear, which he told me he had packed after expressing irritation with me. I was furious that the church had to use benevolent funds to purchase some new drawers for this boy. LAWD!!!

The ministry was instrumental in my children's ability to understand the tenets of baptism and their ability to communicate their decision to get baptized. Taja and Tonja agreed to get baptized on a traditional day, Sunday. On the other hand, Tesha insisted that her baptism take place after her fifth-grade promotion, when her father would be in town and her friends could attend. During this time, Brother Harmon was the senior pastor, and he graciously conducted the baptism on a weekday. He was a bi-vocational pastor who worked the third shift. Once again, Pastor Harmon made another acceptance for another Spires' child on a weekday with an audience of 4th and 5th graders cheering on their friend Jelisa.

The Unbearable Escalation

As a final point, Jay was the only child of mine who had a preset baptism date. I was informed that once he reached the age of nine, he would be ready for baptism. Then I asked, why nine? His reasoning was for him to have a better understanding of why we pray in Jesus' name and not recognize his mother Mary or Moses. I said, that is a very wise question. This was my way of buying myself some time to make an attempt to explain to this six-year-old child that Jesus is the Son of God and the intercession between us and God. Additionally, God selected a pure woman, Mary, to bring forth Jesus, and Moses was directing us to the New Testament, Jesus. Then, Jay tilted his head downward and looked at me over his glasses and said, "Without Mary there would be no Jesus, and without Moses God's children would still be in Egypt?"

In a mirror, I'm sure I looked like I was being asked the answer to the *Jeopardy* question, science for $1,000. I also realized I should attend adult Bible studies more regularly since he tended to pay more attention to the children's Bible stories I read to him. He was baptized five days after making his ninth trip around the sun, on Sunday, February 22, 2004. That evening, he said, "I'm going to meet Jesus when I turn 14 years old."

As soon as I opened my mouth, I gasped for breath. "The only way to meet Jesus in person is to die and leave this earth."

"I'll be okay," he said with such conviction.

At that moment, I knew my prayer life needed to be as confident as Jay's response.

Thinking about it now, it is likely that my children inherited my rash and unique decision-making. In the fifth personal Bible study session with Pastor Jackson and his wife Sister Jackson at my house, I decided to get baptized for the second time. Marion, her parents, Mr. and Mrs. Cooper, and a few church members attended the baptism. It was the first time I really went into the tenets of religious practices such as the Church of Christ and the Church of God in Christ (COGIC).

The two denominations have more similarities than differences. For example, Church of Christ doctrine is derived from the Bible texts for their doctrine and practices, referencing the early Christian church detailed in the New Testament. Most typically, their distinguishing beliefs are that of the necessity of baptism for salvation and the prohibition of instruments in worship. They identify themselves as being non-denominational. In contrast, COGIC is the Holiness-Pentecostal Christian denomination in the U.S. They reject the trinity taught by other denominations and are known as the "Jesus Only" movement. Furthermore, they emphasize divinely inspired powers, such as healing, prophecy, and speaking in tongues.

The first time I was baptized was at the Apostolic Church of Christ, in 1989, under the presiding pastorship of Bishop Brazier. Nevertheless, I identified more strongly with the Church of Christ's doctrine in 2001. Meanwhile, I enjoyed gospel music accompanied by instruments and the congregation singing hymns together. I vividly remember a New Year's Eve when the hymns sounded so angelic and spirit filled.

Then it was time for the Bible Bowl competition between the ladies and the men, including the youth. The angelic voices left the room, replaced by loud, enthusiastic voices and hard slams onto the imaginary buzzer as we pursued the title of Bible Bowl champions. You could've sworn we were trying to win a one-way ticket to Heaven. After the competition, the winners/ladies were bursting with pride that we had earned our bragging rights. Truly, those were joyous times. I used the Bible Bowl to prepare myself for my spiritual journey and future questions from my children, particularly Jay. A part of the preparation was Pastor Harmon's Bible study lessons, such as that a Christian has to be diligent in order to make it in this world. Also, how to pray a successful prayer, for example, "God, enable me to accept your will."

It was an honor for me and my five children to be welcomed into the Dublin Street Church of Christ family. As a result of attending the church, the Spires family was able to grow spiritually and gain biblical knowledge. I will always be grateful.

CHAPTER X

TURNED MY TASSEL

Graduate Studies

It took me three years to complete my undergraduate studies and turn my tassel and walk across the stage at Eastern Illinois University. That same month, I began graduate school. I decided to major in education administration, since I worked at Prairie Elementary School and wanted to be an assistant principal and/or principal.

Graduate school felt like a beautiful disaster. Honestly speaking, I wanted to finish graduate school as soon as possible because I felt this chapter in my life should've been closed at least seven years prior. The school of education was divided into cohorts, so I requested to join various cohorts to speed up the process. The dean granted my request to join the cohorts who met in Danville, Decatur, Vandalia, Mattoon, and Champaign, Illinois. Some courses met three weekends per semester on Friday nights from

5 p.m. to 9 p.m. and Saturdays from 8 a.m. to 5 p.m. I was so determined to finish graduate school, I had to stay in the Ramada Inn in Vandalia. Vandalia, Illinois, is about 2 ½ hours north of Cairo, IL, the last southern city in Illinois. The southern cities' cultures are closely aligned with Upland South rather than with the northern Yankees. Additionally, many southern cities were "sundown towns," meaning black people were not welcome after the sun went down or they would be met with consequences and repercussions—mostly lynching! Also, many sundown towns had code names and dog whistles, like ANNA (Ain't No Nigger Allowed). Basically, this term and practice came about in the late 1890s through the 1970s to keep black people from taking jobs meant for whites, and it also extended to housing policies and policing practices. Now, don't be mistaken, ANNA had a visible presence in northern states and cities as well, such as Arlington Heights and Cicero, Illinois. My parents schooled me and my siblings on this term, "sundown town."[17]

Surprisingly, I had firsthand experience with a sundown town, Valparaiso, Indiana, in the late 1970s. My family took a road trip to drop my sister Jan off at Butternut Springs Girls Scouts' Camp, where she was going to be a camp counselor for the summer. Our green station wagon's front right tire caught a flat on a road in a residential community. My dad told us to get out of the car and stand safely near the left side of the road but not too close to the car. He went to the trunk to retrieve the car jack and lug wrench. Before we knew it, several white people were standing on their front porches with their arms folded and intense stares, like we were the black students of Little Rock Nine trying to integrate into Arkansas' all-white high school. My father used to keep a big stick on the side of the driver's seat just in case of unforeseen circumstances. He told my mama to get the stick and keep watch while he changed the tire. It felt like my dad changed that tire in about 11.5 seconds, like he was a Nascar tire changer. As soon as my daddy finished, he said "Get in," and the whole family jumped in the car as fast as he had switched out the tires. In spite of the knowledge and history I had about ANNA and sundown towns, I was still determined to drive to various towns to acquire my master's degree.

On the way to many classes, Whitney Houston and I would sing a duet of one of her many hits from *The Preacher's Wife* soundtrack and the song "Try It On My Own" on repeat. I was on this tedious journey all by myself without parental support from my children's father. The lyrics rang so true for me:

I'll live my life the way I feel

No matter what

I'm gonna keep it real, you know

It's time for me to do it on my own

So many times, I would cry from the time I put the key in the ignition until I arrived at class in the different cities. I played a lot of music to keep me focused and to keep my spirit from being distressed. At times depression, exhaustion, and the imbalance of life would creep up on me, and it felt too heavy to carry. I talked to myself in between singing "Hold on Help Is on the Way" and "Step by Step." "Paddy, pull up your big girl panties and keep it moving," I said with a quiver in my voice.

On the other hand, some days I was bright-eyed and bushy-tailed and ready to take on the world. In some classes, I had to be a boisterous one like in undergrad because several of my peers were teachers and deans in Central and Southern Illinois, and their educational analysis and unkind comments about predominately black students in their communities and/or schools were biased and damn near racist. I was the only black student in nine of the twelve classes I needed to complete. Sometimes it felt like I had to speak on behalf of the black community, which I welcomed while responding to some of their passive-aggressive comments.

Then my last semester, I completed my practicum at Prairie School and the University of Illinois-Champaign Office of Minority Student Affairs (OMSA) because I became conflicted between secondary education and higher education. The roles of Title I Parent Coordinator and graduate assistant at OMSA both provided me with a parallel experience with black students in secondary and higher education. At the end of the day, they all were working on thriving in an educational system with a 19th-century infrastructure that wasn't structured for black students.

The Shock

"Hello, Adrienne!"

"Hi, Janice!"

"Can you go to Gayle's hotel room so I can talk to the both of you?"

"Sure, I'll be there in about five minutes."

I was thinking Janice wanted to discuss a "Brothas & Sistas" project or the upcoming PTA meeting because I was the vice president. I knocked on Gayle's door, and as soon as I entered

Turned My Tassel

her hotel room the phone rang. Gayle picked up the phone and greeted Janice. Then, Gayle handed me the phone.

I said, "Hello."

Janice said, "Adrienne, you need to come home now. I wanted to make you sure you were with Gayle. I didn't want to tell you this alone. Jeff has been arrested on the alleged charges of sexually abusing your daughter."

That's all I remember hearing Janice saying. Then I hung up the phone.

Gayle looked at me and said, "Adrienne, please don't kill your ex-husband!"

So, I'm assuming the look on my face looked like I was ready to kill. I don't recall if I responded to Gayle. I don't recall my response. I headed to the elevators to go to the lobby to call my sister, DD. She was bringing her children, Jordan and Devin, to visit me while I was in town. The Sheraton Hotel had an old-fashioned telephone booth where you could sit inside and slide the door closed. As I was walking to the phone booth, Dee Dee, Jordan, and Devin entered the lobby. Before I greeted Dee Dee, I broke down crying. I attempted to tell her what had happened. She held me for a moment. I told her what had happened, what was told to me. And she held me again. We went upstairs to let Gayle know my sister was going to drive me home. The ride from downtown Chicago to Homewood to Urbana, IL, usually takes 2½ hours, but it felt like a 5-hour drive to Tennessee.

When we arrived at the house, Jeff was there like nothing ever happened. I said, "Get the hell out of my house!"

He left immediately. My children were scattered around friends' homes because Jeff had come to town to stay with the kids while I attended the conference. Dee Dee spent the night with me and left the next morning. I had to gather all five of my children from their various friends' homes. A case manager from the Department of Children and Family Services (DCFS) called to schedule a time to meet in person to talk about the alleged child sexual abuse report and the next steps in the process. I asked the case manager why Jeff hadn't been arrested. She stated the report was an alleged child sexual abuse case. By this time, it was assumed Jeff had left town and gone back to Chicago.

The same day, my children and I had to attend a meeting at Champaign County's Children's Advocacy Center (CAC). My daughter was interviewed a couple of days before my other children by CAC staff. I had a roundtable meeting with the investigation team from various child serving systems, such as DCFS, CAC, Champaign County Mental Health Center, a pediatric doctor from Carle Hospital, Champaign County Sheriff's Department, and Champaign County District Attorney's Office's Victim Advocacy Services for them to share what they had learned from my daughter's interviews. In addition, they expounded on the purpose of and process to receive coordinated and comprehensive services for my daughter, her siblings, and me as her custodial parent.

CHAPTER XI

INDUCTED INTO THE NON-OFFENDING PARENT CLUB

The Trauma

After all of the formalities and pleasantries, the meeting began. Unanimously, the investigation team agreed my daughter's timeline of the abuse that took place at home and my whereabouts during the heinous acts were consistent. Thousands of emotions were swirling in my mind like a swarm of locusts while I sat at the table that resembled a table of judges. Each team member disclosed the facts found during their conversation with my daughter. The conversation was an actual interview facilitated by a specially trained forensic interviewer who poses non-leading questions to children to tell their side of the story. One of the overwhelming disclosures was that she decided to tell her friend at school after her biological father attempted to put his mouth on her "private part" (vagina) and climb on top of her. According to her, this was the first time he went that far, and she had never experienced this new kind of fear. While sitting in my assigned seat and listening to the one investigator verbalize the collective account to all in attendance, I distinctly recall feeling like a character in a Spike Lee movie in a double dolly shot; the effect makes characters seem as if they are floating down a street rather than walking. Then it was like an out-of-body experience, where I was watching myself in a damn unreal scene from the television show *The Twilight Zone*. Someone at the table asked if I needed a break. I said something to the effect of, "No, thank you." Some of the faces seemed surprised and looked away after my response. When I was younger, we used to play the "staring game," and the first person who blinked or looked away was deemed the loser. Actually, the object of the game was to see if one had confidence in themselves. If a poker face had any monetary value, I would've been a millionaire. I really wanted to fall apart, but my "poker face" dictated otherwise.

After the grief session that posed as a meeting, I was adamant about killing that negro, Jeff! In retrospect, did I welcome the devil's influence to become calculating with a nefarious smile about my ex-husband's future, or was I a wounded lioness who didn't protect her cub?

Jeff had said, "I don't want us to depend on other people watching the kids. Let's work opposite shifts to avoid childcare since they're so young."

All the while, the babysitter from hell lived within. The meeting played in my head at least a thousand times a day. Before the meeting closed, I was asked, "Do you have any questions or any concerns."

I only had questions for myself. How did I miss this? Why didn't she feel like she could tell me? How can I kill him, and can I get off with temporary insanity? This horrendous situation took me to an extremely dark place where I was premeditating murder to avenge the unspeakable act inflicted on my daughter. At that point, I truly believed "the only way to reform people (Jeff) is to kill 'em" (Carl Panzram, who claimed to have committed 21 murders and over a thousand rapes and was executed in 1930). Murder was never a part of my spirit, but it was influential to my temporary mindset. Let me say to non-offending parents who have envisioned revenge: You're not crazy. You had a normal response to an abnormal situation, and your reaction was valid given the familial member's unfathomable action.

Even as a domestic violence victim, I never thought about committing murder. I was always in a defensive and escape mode. This time was different; it was "the race of life." The story of the lion and the gazelle. Every morning, the gazelle had to arise early to avoid being eaten by the lion. The lion had to arise early to avoid starving to death. Every day, I was thinking, pondering, and plotting how I would win this race in this lifetime. This goes to show a mother's love is indescribable and greater than infinity. It was totally out of character … or was it?

The investigation team defined child sexual abuse (CSA) as any interaction between a child and an adult (or another child) in which the child is used for the sexual stimulation of the perpetrator or an observer. "Sexual abuse can include both touching and non-touching behaviors. Non-touching behaviors can include voyeurism (trying to look at a child's naked body), exhibitionism, or exposing the child to pornography. Children of all ages, races, ethnicities, and economic backgrounds may experience sexual abuse. Child sexual abuse affects both girls and boys in all kinds of neighborhoods and communities."[18]

I heard family and church members quote the scripture, *"Dearly beloved, avenge not yourselves, but rather give place unto wrath: for it is written, Vengeance is mine; I will repay, saith the Lord"* (Romans 12:19, KJV). I heard this verse repeatedly throughout my childhood and adulthood. Some people used it as an affirmation or a way to convince themselves not to take matters into their own hands or become a judge and jury. I convinced myself I wasn't being vengeful but a responsible mother protecting the welfare of my child. I believe God knew there would be some unimaginable acts that would cause the humblest, most faithful, and meekest to step outside their spiritual character.

I would have preferred to learn about child sexual abuse through a professional training and/or a book chosen by a book club. However, my preference was not solicited nor considered. The only abuse I was familiar with was being a domestic violence victim, nothing about child sexual abuse and/or childhood trauma. On top of that, I was reluctantly inducted into the "non-offending parent" club. The term non-offending parent refers to a parent or caregiver who has not been involved in the sexual assault, is intra-familial, and the offender is an uncle, brother, grandfather, or other relative. Both parents can be described as non-offending. Sadly, Jeff was the offender.[19] When I divorced Jeff, I felt I had left the lion's den. Then, I learned my daughter had been suffering in his secret lion's den.

In addition to everything else, I had two overlapping traumas, as a victim of domestic violence and as a non-offending parent. Then, I did some research about the two coexisting tragedies. What I uncovered was devastating. There was an overlap between domestic violence and incest perpetrators. Incest perpetrators were four to six times more likely to sexually abuse their children and batter the mother of their children. Some more disturbing behaviors they exhibit are manipulation, psychological abuse, and cruelty.[20] The research and unsettling behaviors described Jeff perfectly, such as his constant threats to harm me, insults, and gaslighting. As a victim of domestic violence, I never fathomed our children were in harm's way and most definitely did not imagine that one of them could be a victim of incest.

At the time, I wasn't aware of the study of "intersectionality": the interconnected nature of social categorizations such as race, class, and gender as they apply to a given individual or group, regarded as creating overlapping and interdependent systems of discrimination or disadvantage (Wikipedia). This analytical framework was coined in 1989 by Dr. Kimberlé Crenshaw. Professor Crenshaw is a leading scholar of Critical Race Theory and full-time law professor at UCLA and Columbia Law School. Strangely, the nature of my life identified with the interconnection of all the social disadvantages of intersectionality, such as domestic violence victim/survivor, non-offending parent, single/divorced mother, nontraditional college student, and being of a lower socioeconomic status (SES).

In the meantime, a Champaign County Sheriff Deputy called me to share the name and contact information for the detective at the Chicago Police Department's Child Advocacy Division who would be working the case from Chicago. I contacted Detective Wells and did the formal introduction. I inquired about the next steps concerning Jeff. He stated he had scheduled a time and date to meet with him to conduct an interview about the situation. I was infuriated with Detective Wells' response. Calmly, I said, "I must admit I haven't had law since my junior year of high school. I don't remember anyone with a national warrant could schedule a time to meet with a detective." He said, "Pardon me. There's a national warrant for his arrest for child sexual abuse. Let me rephrase that: alleged child sexual abuse, according to the Department of Child Family Services (DCFS)." I said, "I can retrieve a copy of the national warrant from the Champaign County Circuit Clerk's website."

My friend Shandra and I searched the website and found the warrant as easy as saying 1, 2, 3. I forwarded the copy of the summons with a message asking him to please call when it arrived. Detective Wells called me about two days later to inform me that when he had arrived at the address Jeff provided, guess what, Jeff wasn't there. Then I inquired about the address and asked who answered the door. Unsurprisingly, my ex-mother-in-law had greeted the detective and stated he had just missed Jeff. How convenient! Detective Wells kept me abreast of Jeff's case and comforted me with the assurance he would do everything he could to adhere to the warrant.

Finally, Jeff was apprehended in Chicago at the beginning of June 2005. He was detained and placed in Cook County Department of Corrections until transferred to the Champaign County Department of Corrections. Reluctantly, I had to go visit Jeff at the Champaign County Jail because our oldest daughter,

Taja, had run away from home. To be on the safe side, I made a missing person report at the Champaign County Sheriff's Department. The trauma had taken an emotional toll on all of my children. My first thought was she went to Chicago, where the majority of our family resided. Ironically, after my visit with Jeff, it was confirmed, she was at his sister's house. The same sister who was unfamiliar with her whereabouts when I first inquired. Jeff remained in the county jail for about three months.

Telling the Whole Truth, So Help Me God

I distinctly remember my first meeting with the victim advocate from the Champaign County District Attorney's Office and the assistant district attorney (DA). The meeting started with, "You and Jeff Spires are divorced. Correct? While married you had a couple of domestic disputes."

I said, "That is correct."

They had a condescending tone throughout the meeting.

"Your daughter stated you were not present during the time of the abuse by the hands of her father. Oh, Ms. Spires, you are a graduate student at Eastern Illinois University, majoring in education administration. And once upon a time, Bank One, located on Mattis Avenue and Springfield Ave in Champaign, which had business hours from 7 a.m.-midnight. You worked the 4 p.m.-midnight shift during the week and some weekends."

The imaginary speech bubble above my head said, "No shit, Sherlock!"

The assistant DA asked, "Are you serving another term as the vice-president of the PTA at Prairie Elementary School this year?"

My mild mannered but curt response was, "Not this school year."

I refused to partake in any appeasement. I felt like I was being investigated more than Jeff, and he was the actual perpetrator. It appeared they were a little taken aback that this young black divorced mother of five children was in graduate school and that my kids were enrolled in various academic and extracurricular activities hosted by the University of Illinois Champaign-Urbana campus.

The fact that my dossier and whereabouts was the main topic of discussion confirmed stereotypical analysis that disqualifies me as a black woman from being a "perfect victim" of domestic violence, sexual assault, and as a non-offending parent, actually any victim. The "perfect victim" must display ladylike characteristics by wearing clothing not too short or revealing, have a pristine past, and "report the crime perfectly," for example, chronically and consistently. Sadly, black women find their reports disbelieved because of racist narratives that cast them as hypersexual or undesirable.[21]

At the time, I was quite disappointed I was being viewed as a potential co-conspirator or a neglector and not as the concerned mother of an abused minor trying to get justice. By this time, my analysis of this particular institution was that the more things change, the more they remain the same. The same actions are read differently. Being an articulate foe of injustice may be seen as a praiseworthy trait among whites; however, black women with similar traits may be seen as bitter, selfish complainers, also known as the angry black woman. Such comparisons derived from the Sapphire Caricature that portrays black women as stubborn, rude, loud, malicious, and overbearing.

Inducted Into the Non-Offending Parent Club

At the second meeting, my daughter and I met with the victim advocate and the assistant DA. We were told my daughter would have to testify in the courtroom. Then, I asked if there was a way she could give her testimony via video because she didn't want to see her dad in the courtroom.

The assistant DA said, "No."

Excuse me, have I been watching too much Law & Order SVU? I was under the impression children's testimonies could be recorded and used as evidence in the court. Sad to say, that wasn't an option. Consequently, the presumed process proved inaccurate. He said we could have her chair positioned where she wouldn't be able to see him in the courtroom. She turned her head left to right slowly several times. That was a gesture of no. I supported her decision. As a result, the case couldn't move forward without an actual testimony in the courtroom, per the assistant DA. She went to the waiting room so we could wrap up the meeting. The advocate, the assistant DA, and I discussed the impact of intra-familial child sexual abuse on children. According to their experience and some research, the child may be fearful of the perpetrators and potential verbal threats toward family members. Furthermore, testifying may cause her to re-experience the trauma and cause extreme anxiety.[22]

At the closing of the meeting, the victim advocate stated "According to the State of Illinois statute of limitations Public Act 1000-0080, your daughter has 20 years after she reaches age 18, or five years after the discovery that sexual abuse occurred and caused injuries."[23] My daughter's therapists totally agreed with the research, recommendation, and her decision. This whole damn ordeal was so disheartening to me. I thought I had to come up with a new deal for me and my babies.

No charges were brought against Jeff since our daughter wasn't comfortable testifying in his presence.

After the assistant DA's and the court's decision, I went to a darker place in my life. I was more broken than previously, but I didn't believe I could feel any lower. I thought pitch black was the blackest. I decree and declare the dark path I experienced surpassed pitch black. Slowly, I strategized to regain Jeff's trust by displaying a submissive and longing characteristic. Jeff was a person who yearned for power and control and was drawn to submission and desire. Erotically, I was willing to give him everything he thought he wanted and then some.

It started with sporadic conversations I initiated, such as, "How are you adapting to the Windy City?"

I remembered when we used to hang out at 31st Street Beach and Navy Pier. The more sporadic the calls, the more he wanted to converse about old times. Approximately three months later, I turned up the romantic gestures and subtle invitations. Historically, our love life was the opposite of coy. He welcomed my alluring propositions, and I was pleased with my splendid performances. I never took a drama course in my many years of schooling. We met in Chicago on a brisk October evening. The evening was filled with the "darkest passions" and "erotic fiction," like a scene from Zane's book *The Sex Chronicles*.

My sole purpose for luring Jeff was to kill him. I gave up a piece of me to get him to be vulnerable. In actuality, I became a modern-day Delilah in the biblical story of Samson and Delilah (Judges

Inducted Into the Non-Offending Parent Club

16). She was a Philistine who, bribed to entrap Samson, coaxed him into revealing that the secret of his strength was his long hair, whereupon she took advantage of his confidence to betray him to his enemies. Her name has since become synonymous with a voluptuous, treacherous woman.[24] (http://www.,britannica.com/biography/Delilah) In 2005, ignorance was bliss for me about getting away with murder, and this lasted until 2012, when I started working in the anti-gender-based violence field. At the time, I was under the incorrect impression that defending myself would have sufficed for a homicide or self-defense. Rightfully so, as there were documented orders of protections, 911 calls, being a domestic violence victim, and being a non-offending parent.

Horrifyingly, in 2012, a young black woman named Marissa Alexander, who had a restraining order and other documented history of domestic violence by the hands of her then-husband, was convicted of aggravated assault and sentenced to a mandatory minimum 20 years behind bars. Marissa had fired a warning shot at her husband in an encounter in her Jacksonville, FL, home. The court denied her the opportunity to utilize the stand-your-ground defense. Marissa's trial took place the same year George Zimmerman, who murdered Trayvon Martin, was found not guilty because of the stand-your-ground defense. Alexander believes "the current burden of proof, formalized in a 2015 state Supreme Court decision, gives the government too much power and criminalizes domestic violence victims—black women in particular.[25]"

Meanwhile, my children and I were going to family counseling and individual counseling and were fulfilling schedules from before the trauma took place. We were exhausted! Only the daughter who was abused and I liked our sessions with our therapists. My other four children didn't find any significance with their outreach counselors. My abused daughter continued to see her therapist for a year. She expressed several years later that she appreciated the way her therapist respected her as a young lady.

Means of Escape, Sensual Distraction

So, it is May 2005, shortly after my entanglement with the court system and child servicing systems began. One of my best friends, Dr. Major Kim, who was attending graduate school at Bradley University in Peoria, Illinois, invited me to attend a black fraternity cruise party. Many people from surrounding areas and some from afar attended this annual cruise.

The cruise was so well attended that my friend Shandra was walking around the boat to verify if there were enough life jackets and getaway boats in case of a shipwreck and/or emergency. She said, "There are a lot of black folks boarding this cruise, and you know our swimming skills are a little scary." Between me and you, I believe she was a little traumatized from the movie *Titanic*. She wasn't sure if the men on the boat would assist her onto the lifeboat or throw her overboard. According to research, 70 percent of black folks can't swim; a lack of access to public pools and a history of segregated swimming have kept many of them out of the water.[26]

Finally, the unsolicited inventory was completed.

So, we swayed to the beat of the music into the party. We were able to cop a couple of front row seats to the dance floor. Right before my very eyes, there was a tall drink of water dancing with a young lady. Subtly, I inquired, "Who's that?"

Nonchalantly, Shandra gave me the scoop on this unfamiliar face. Then, she gave me a look like only Ms. Juicy from *The Rickey Smiley Radio Show* could give. You are "shady," with a side eye and slow head turn at the same time. Next, we burst into breathtaking laughter.

The night continued with fraternity chants and rump shaking to Lil John's "Get Low" (to the window to the wall). A cute young lady was dancing with one of the fraternity guys to "Get Low." Let's just say burlesque dancers, the Las Vegas Rockettes, and erotic dancers couldn't compete with her. Ironically, black fraternities are known for their precision stepping moves, but he was so mesmerized, he looked more like Peewee Herman than a guy who perfected stepping with a cane. No disrespect intended, just a fun and memorable moment.

The night closed with a visit to Perkin Restaurant with late-night shenanigans and a sleepover at Kim's place. The very next morning, we hit I-74 East heading back to Champaign-Urbana to get ourselves and our children ready for church. There is an old saying in the black community, "If you can go out on a Saturday night, you can get to church on a Sunday morning."

It was time to get back to reality. I greeted "blue Monday" with the gospel song "I Need You To Survive" by Hezekiah Walker & The Love Fellowship Choir. Per usual, my morning continued to start off with some much-needed inspiration. Approximately a week later, my friend Janice, the founder of the Brothas and Sistas Program hosted at Prairie Elementary School, invited me and two of my daughters to attend the Champaign County

Mental Health Board meeting with her to ask for funding for the Black History Museum and tour to Windsor and Dresden, Canada. My daughters had been honorary members of Brothas and Sistas since they were four and six years old. After Janice spoke on behalf of the program, I stretched a little bit, and who did I see in the audience? The "tall glass of water" from the cruise. After the meeting was adjourned, Janice and I walked out to the corridor to debrief. Then, Janice introduced me and the "tall glass water" and stated the organization he led as executive director.

Casually, I said, "Nice to meet you. How ironic. I have been trying to connect with your organization about scholarships for College for Kids. Unfortunately, the program director hasn't got back to me yet."

He was like, "Really?"

He pulled out his Blackberry and texted the program director. He assured me I would receive a call within a couple of days. Sadly, a couple of days turned into three days. I had to do my due diligence and make a follow-up call to the executive director: "Good afternoon, I still haven't heard anything from the mysterious program director you texted last week. Are you sure you texted the correct number?"

At first, he chuckled, and then, in his distinguished voice, he said, "I have the correct contact information in my phone."

"Whew, good. I thought maybe you were trying to ditch Prairie School and keep all the scholarships for your organizations."

Then, he said "I will cc you on the email to Peter" (in the back of my mind, the mysterious program director). "Is it Ms. or Mrs. Spires?"

I said, "Ms. Spires."

I heard the slight grin in his voice. Then, the coy conversation began.

The call ended with him so kindly asking, "Can you please keep me abreast of the students who receive scholarships?"

I said, "Absolutely. And have a good day."

A couple of days had passed when he called me at work to inquire if I was pleased with Peter's assistance.

My response: "Peter was as helpful as he could be."

Then, the real question was posed, if he could call me outside of work hours on my cell phone.

"Currently, a cell isn't within my budget."

He said, "Pardon me?"

"I'm a full-time student."

"Do you attend Parkland Community College?"

"No, I'm in graduate school at Eastern Illinois University."

The small talk led to him asking me out to dinner. I selected the place to meet. He exhibited well-mannered characteristics. However, I didn't know this man from Adam. As a result, I selected the restaurant Kennedy's at Stone Creek located on the Stone Creek Golf Club.

I always put forth a concerted effort to be punctual, and it was fulfilled this time. I arrived at 5:50 p.m. for a 6 p.m. date. He was a tad bit late, with an arrival time of 6:10 p.m. He apologized profusely for his tardiness and said, "It will never happen again." Well, I didn't have a cell phone for him to inform me he would be late. In the back of my mind, I was thinking, he assumes there will be another date. Well, this negro is confident.

The hostess took us to our table. I said, "I wasn't sure if you would recognize me since my hair is braided instead of my bob hairstyle."

With an admiring grin, he said, "I recognize your dimples."

Then, I lowered my smile to show my dimples. The old saying goes, don't give it all at once, then there's nothing to look forward to (or you become overfamiliar).

"Oh, so I noticed you had brought your two daughters to the Mental Health Board meetings. Do you just have two children?"

I said, "Oh no, I have five children."

He paused and looked a little stunned.

Candidly, he posed another question, "Do they all have the same father?"

I readjusted my posture. I said, "Well, I'm not sure what type of women you are used to being in the presence of, but all my children have the same biological father, and we were married once upon a time."

He looked perplexed and then slowly nodded his head.

My response to his nod was, "If you stick with me, you will wish you were the father of my children."

I knew I probably should have left, and I don't know why I stayed. Looking back on that moment, I saw him as a stallion that needed to be broken. I was engrossed with the challenge to validate my strength.

A new conversation started with me stating, "I asked around about you. I heard you're not married."

He replied, "But I am engaged."

At that point, I reciprocated his nod. A moment of silence entered our space.

"Ex … cu … se me, I need to go to the ladies' room."

Swiftly, I walked to the restroom and called my friend. I said, "Oh my God, he's engaged! I need to leave right now."

"He's not married," she remarked.

"Girl, bye!"

With hesitation, I returned to the table.

He led the conversation with "What are you studying at EIU?"

With an enamored grin, "Education administration."

Gently, he leaned in with a focused gaze. It was as if we were the only two in Kennedy's. I expounded on my theory of education: "Never allow one educational institution to solely educate you and/or your kids, especially if you are black."

"Exactly, he replied!"

The chat covered politics, economics (e.g. the International Monetary Fund), and different genres of music. For example, Chicago styles of music, such as house and stepping. R. Kelly's name entered into the conversation because he is a native of Chicago. His current hit was "In the Kitchen." "No, absolutely not!" "Mannish covers will not dominate this dinner date," I said, tilting my head to the right. Amidst smirks and amused stares, the convo went back to substance, for instance, being reared in all-black communities in Chicago and Alabama. At times, it felt like we were having a roundtable discussion, and it lasted for approximately three hours. Dialogues with substance are intriguing to me. They're damn near erotic.

The stars and moon were shining brightly on this crisp night as I was escorted to my van. Once we arrived at the door on the driver's side, he leaned in to give me a hug and/or kiss. My right hand was extended. "Thank you for dinner and an engaging discussion," I concluded.

This date was the introduction to my "means of escape," aka Maurice. I didn't feel the world's weight on my shoulders with this individual, and my traumas were not displayed like fishbowls while with him.

Kennedy's at Stone Creek was graced with our presence for the second date. We conversed about black cinema, such as *Cooley High* and "the great state of Alabama Roll Tide football team," March Madness, and my future goals to run a 5k and hopefully a marathon. My sister friend, Dr. Major Kim's participation in a Chicago marathon in 1998 inspired my dream of running a marathon one day. Maurice and my interactions led to a nontraditional, unprecedented relationship for approximately ten years.

The relationship was metaphoric, light but heavy, riddled with complications, temporary, with no expiration date, and a poisonous cure. But it was pretty convenient for me then and felt so right.

I was perfectly content with a few phone calls during the week and bi-weekly lunch dates at my home because I was so busy as a divorced mom of five children, dealing with child servicing systems and the courts, being employed full-time, and as a full-time graduate student.

Simultaneously, our conversations became more consistent along with our standing lunch dates. It was so needed since my life resembled a person with a dual personality. I wanted to dissociate with the direct trauma thrusted on my daughter and myself and its lingering effect on my other children, and to not identify with Adrienne/Paddy, who was the domestic violence victim/survivor, non-offending parent, and whose coping mechanism was intentional busyness to avoid the matters at hand. He wasn't aware of what my children and I were enduring. I was in a totally different place when I was with him. It was like a relaxing stroll through the Japanese Friendship Gardens at Balboa Park in San Diego, CA, and the Master Gardens of Champaign County Extension Unit with their blooming cherry blossom plants, bamboo trees, and purple lilac flowers.

Not looking back at the dark past and just walking into the brightness the future had to offer me. I was still able to be my outgoing self and reserved when I deemed it necessary. Ultimately, rage was buried within me, and sometimes I felt it simmering. "I sat with my anger long enough until she told me her real name was grief" (C.S. Lewis). Internally, I resembled *Melancholy*, a sculpture created by Albert Gyorgy, that portrays the void that grief leaves us with. "The sculpture depicts a figure made of copper sitting on a bench slumped over, with a giant hole in the center of it. This hole represents the massive void that we all feel when we lose someone dear to us" [27]

I grieved over the loss of my daughter' and her siblings' childhood and innocence. Some things that are lost in life can't be recovered even with the best therapy and the very best motherly intentions.

CHAPTER XII

THE PSYCHOLOGICAL PROCESS

Individual Counseling

I met with my daughter's therapist, Judy. It was one of the best interactions I have ever had with a therapist. We had a conversation; she talked with me, not to me. There were no elephants in the room, archetypes, stereotypes, and "You are such a strong black woman"—eye roll.

We discussed the protection I had to provide for my daughter and the fragile emotional state of the other children. Judy expressed her concerns for the massive undertaking of emotional capacity and delicacy needed for all the children and myself. Before the meeting ended, Judy highly recommended I meet with a therapist for support.

I started therapy with Connie in the summer of 2005 and continued until the fall of 2009. I needed some balance in my life. I felt like Clark Kent rushing to change from his business suit into his Superman cape, except I had to wear multiple capes trying to normalize five children's traumatized lives. My ultimate goal was to be mentally stable. At the same time, I was thinking about committing a homicide. It was one of my daily affirmations. I was calm, without any emotions, not a sense of empathy in the world. And I was perfectly okay with that particular cape, as I said to Connie.

Connie would see how overwhelmed I was when I entered her office.

"Hey, your way of dealing with trauma is to stay busy. You move too fast; you move constantly, and you're not taking time to assess the trauma you have endured, and you're not resting."

She continued, saying, "I am afraid that your coping mechanisms will cause you to crash and burn one day. You're not going to be able to continue to handle your trauma in this manner."

So, I listened intently. However, I couldn't slow down because I was responsible for saving myself and my children.

I appreciated that Connie helped me better understand that my behaviors and my thoughts were driven by unconscious meanings and motivations. For a moment, I thought I was going crazy. Those four years with Connie and my prayer life introduced me to the journey of healing.

Faith & Spiritual Guidance

It was May 2005. I had finished graduate school and started a new career at the Mental Health Center of Champaign County. I was hired as a home visitor and was promoted to teen parent coordinator shortly after. The abuse was still fresh in my mind in light of the new opportunities. During this time, I had a couple of conversations with one of my former EIU classmates, Sylvia. She suggested I visit her church, Center of Hope's, prayer services on Wednesday and Friday mornings from 5 a.m. to 6 a.m. The ministry was led by Apostle Robert Smith and First Lady Cassandra Smith. That was another spiritual introduction for me. I attended the Center of Hope prayer ministry for about eight years, and my faith grew. It helped me throughout the days and the nights of crying, feeling frustrated, and wanting to commit a homicide and keep it together for my children simultaneously. The prayer sessions and ministry never failed me. It showed me God was real and God was not a man. God's angels and disciples were always available to comfort me. Prayer would start with a gospel song(s) with the chilling effect of Pentecost, with the four main parts of a choir: soprano, alto, tenor, and bass, while singing acapella, "Jesus is the Lighthouse."

A good prayer session always opens the floor for testimonies on how God's promises and blessings are still relevant today. The saints gave testimonies about family members on death's doorstep and a banana peel slip away from being evicted or a pink slip. One of the most touching was when a cancer patient's survival rate was less than 25%, but they lived an additional five years as if every day was their last.

The engine in my minivan had died and needed to be replaced during a Midwest winter. First Lady Smith picked me up every Wednesday and Friday at 4:35 a.m. for two months when Jack Frost nipped at our noses. Don't get me wrong; I was not a holy roller, as some people will call it. There were so many mornings when I was exhausted and didn't want to get out of bed at the crack of dawn. But I knew there were only two times to pray: When you want to, and when you don't want to.

During these eight years, I became a gleeful grandmother to Brandon, Jada, and Gracie.

One of my heartfelt prayer requests stemmed from my two granddaughters, Jada and Gracie. They were so excited when I bought them Doc McStuffins bubble bath. They stayed in the tub so long their skin started to resemble the California raisins from the commercial in the 1980s. I was becoming tired just from monitoring them for about 45 minutes. I kept extending the bath time an extra five minutes. The only way for me not to add another five minutes was to remove the stopper. Jada and Gracie slid through the tub until the last bubble dissolved. Watching them relish in the bubbles made me wish all children could access clean water and extended bath time. Unfortunately, water is viewed as a luxury by some, such as citizens of sub-Saharan Africa, and as an essential by others. The article "Dying for a Drink" sheds light on unclean and diseased water in countries on the continent of Africa. In contrast, other continents' water sources are drinkable without disease threats.

How in the HELL was this even an issue? The song "We Are the World" was number one on the Billboard charts, and hundreds of millions of dollars were raised for Africa. My prayer request was for people to quench for water but never thirst. That prayer led me to advocate for clean water globally with a Christian nongovernmental organization called World Vision. Some of the biggest requests stemmed from social ills, headlines ripped from newspapers, and populations we worked with and for. I requested prayers for the teen mothers I worked with in the teen parent program. I prayed for their spirit and souls not to be broken by people who should love and protect them as well as the systems established to do so. All I could do at times was lift my hands, and my tears would flow downward. Cognitively, I was shouting and praising God as loud as possible while requesting to be held safe in his arms. The teen moms and I needed the same spiritual protection.

I spent two hours per week for 52 weeks over eight years, which equals 832 hours, being in the presence of God and sending up prayers. I am a witness; they helped me when I least expected, and sometimes I felt my prayers were unheard as a non-offending parent. As I reminisce about the early stages of my prayer experiences, it equates to one of Dr. Rev. Otis Moss's sermons, "Do Not Fall in Despair at This Moment." The gist of the sermon was, "Until we are faced with the lowest moment, we don't realize how much power is in us," and we're "caught between pain and possibility." I had made up my mind, yes, I will trust God. Sending my love to Sylvia, Apostle Smith, and Sister Smith for obeying God and hearing my soul cries.

CHAPTER XIII

"IT'S EASIER TO BUILD STRONG CHILDREN THAN TO REPAIR BROKEN MEN"- FREDRICK DOUGLASS

Introducing Teen Mothers to Their Own Expertise, 2006-2009

During the first three months as a home visitor, I worked with a child's family to ensure that the home environment supported their education. As a home visitor, I spent time with the mother and her baby too.

So, I became a home visitor with the Early Childhood Mental Health Development department's program Healthy Young Families (HYF) at the mental health center in Champaign County. I was a home visitor, where I visited teen moms who live with other family members raising their infants and toddlers. The purpose was to help ensure that their children would develop as they should. The program also introduced different activities to stimulate their brains because children from zero to five years old have brains like sponges; they soak up everything. They are at the age where they're so impressionable. They also learn quickly. Then, within three months, I was promoted to the teen parent group coordinator, so I facilitated groups twice a week on Tuesdays and Thursdays for different sets of teen moms. I also worked with the home visitors so they would get the teen moms to be a part of the support groups. In the support groups, we talked about a lot of subjects especially for them to bond and connect with their children. So the support groups would start with a parent-child activity. The HYF team was "kick ass": Tasha, Keona, and Erin. We were a well-oiled machine. The volunteers and interns were just as committed as us. As a team, we created a setting for families.

Every session started with a sit-down dinner followed by a parent-child activity. Then, we would address subject matter like avoiding subsequent births, but we also wanted to make sure they graduated from high school. We made sure they knew that they were experts when it came to their children.

My affirmation at meetings was, "You're all that and a little bit more."

I wanted it to penetrate their souls because this world is not geared towards embracing and building black women's worth. I had grown to love these moms, especially since my daughters were in the same age group. Aside from being intelligent, witty, funny, caring, and wise, they also had a good sense of humor. And so, with this particular program, this was an opportunity for them to choose how they wanted to raise their children, how they wanted to bond with their children, and how they wanted to move in their life career-wise, education-wise, family-wise, and as black mothers.

We wanted to encourage them, and I appreciated this program. So, we saw some funding from the mental health center, but we would see the bulk of our funding from the Ounce of Prevention Fund in Chicago and Springfield. This was an opportunity to lead these young mothers, and also we had a fathers initiative program. I also co-facilitated Family Administered Neonatal Activities (FANA) and a prenatal group with a labor and delivery nurse at Carle Hospital in Urbana, Illinois. It was for the community's teen moms, dads, and other women.

Some mothers-to-be shared how some perinatal health providers were rude and wouldn't explain medical terms they used during visits. In addition, any discomfort they asked about, they were reassured, "It's normal." The now Stacy Grundy, DrPH, who volunteered with HYF while in undergrad at the U of I, suggested writing prenatal term definitions on construction paper, laminating them, and placing them on key chains. This was so they could reference them during their visits. For example, "episiotomy." We were furious that their presence and inquiries were being dismissed and annoyed. On occasion, home visitors accompanied the participants to prenatal visits for emotional support and as advocates. They really needed doulas. A doula serves as a person experienced in childbirth who provides advice, information, and emotional support and who offers mental and physical comfort during and immediately after childbirth (National Black Doula Association). Unfortunately for Champaign County, doula services were only offered to the HYF programs in Chicago and other regions of the state. While in training with doulas, I learned that similar experiences were common among low-income teenage clients who were black or Mexican.

The HYF group offered so many other enlightening experiences that lead to laughter, reflection, anticipation, and growth. One support group session, Dr. Robin Orr taught us exercises to work both sides of our brains by moving our arms in different directions. I felt like I was trying to chew gum, tap the top of my head, and rub my belly simultaneously. It was a difficult task for me and some of the moms. We appeared discombobulated with two left arms. My coworker Keona mastered the activity. Honestly, I know only one side for me was stimulated. I believe we looked so bad throughout the exercise that it prompted Dr. Orr to say, "Dancing is good for the brain."

So, I took it to the next level and invited a U of I hip-hop dance team, "Conglomerate," to rescue us and teach us some hip moves while discreetly connecting the brain. Couldn't nobody tell us we were not practicing for Missy Elliot's music video, "Lose Control."

Most of the group sessions encompassed my favorite three pillars of life: information, resources, and exposure to different life experiences and cultures. The Healthy Young Families team made sure the participants were encouraged and talked with not talked down to.

With all of that, we had some of the best times encouraging these young women and letting them know that they were the experts of their children and that we respected them. One of the most profound parts of this program was the "Heart to Heart" training that I had to go through. This particular training was to help teen moms prevent child sexual abuse because, unfortunately, most teen moms are homeless. I say "homeless" to mean that their name is not on the lease where they reside, even if they reside with their parents, other family members, or friends.

The matriarch tends to help lead and facilitate how parenting should be. And there are some things that the matriarchs are unfamiliar with, as shown in new studies. For example, the risk of sudden infant death syndrome (SIDS) means that you shouldn't have your baby sleeping with you. This is because the heat from the two adults that may be sleeping in a bed with the baby may become overheated. It is also necessary to make sure the baby sleeps on their back and not on their stomach. And just things like that, not to be disrespectful to the matriarch, but we wanted to teach the new research regarding children's mental health.

Also, the "Heart to Heart" program. This 12-week program is very, very intense. Teaching teen moms how to protect their babies from child sexual abuse and the multiple impacts on children's development, as well as journal writing and a community project. Each participant had to select "Heartmates," who are people who would pledge to support them after they completed the program. Just as much as the participants, I needed the program. To get through the ordeal my children and I were undergoing at that time, I needed several "Heartmates!"

The program also discusses the various effects of childhood sexual abuse on child development and childbearing, the effects of abuse on female adolescents' sexuality and their capacity to learn, and the role of poverty in this issue.

While I was co-facilitating the "Heart to Heart" curriculum for teen mothers, about 90% of the participants disclosed they were victims of child sexual abuse. The perpetrators were school teachers, the mother's boyfriends, aunts and uncles, and clergy. There were many times my heart almost stopped while listening to the disclosures. One of the mother's boyfriends went into the bathroom while the teen mom was nude multiple times. The straw that broke the camel's back for the participant was the fifth time he "mistakenly" entered her room after she got out of the shower. She went and told her mother, and, unfortunately, she sided with her boyfriend. The participant said while crying, "She let him stay and told me it was an accident." Then the boyfriend had the audacity to display a smirk on his face like, now what are you going to do? In the back of my mind, I thought, "You low-down bastard."

Another participant's aunt was on crack cocaine and prostituted her in exchange for drugs. When she told her mother, the aunt said she was "lying" and just a "fast tail girl." She shared the tragedy with a trusted school counselor who would later have her meet him at a restaurant to make her feel safe. Then, she could barely speak when she proceeded to tell us that one particular day, he convinced her to meet him at a remote location, where he sexually assaulted her. She then placed a piece of paper in front of her face to avoid displaying her agony. She went as far as to say, "I should've known better."

These stories were shared at the same group meeting. All I could think of was wanting to kill the counselor, the boyfriend, and my ex-husband. I felt the same about the aunt and screamed loudly, in my mind, "Sorry-ass excuse for a woman!"

I took their stories and unfortunate experiences to the prayer group—*"the prayer of a righteous man availeth much"* (James 5:16,

KJV). For me to continue to co-facilitate with strength and supportive listening, only God's grace and mercy could carry me through.

My office was the "secret place of prayer" for the Black Healthy Young Families team because we wanted the very best outcomes for the young mothers and knew the daily challenges they were facing. One particular day, Tasha and I prayed about her starting her own 501c (3) for teen mothers. The organization was established and successfully helped many teen mothers in Champaign County, Illinois, to reach some goals beyond their imagination. Additionally, some of the other black staff came to the "secret place of prayer" about their clients, systemic practices, and professional aspirations.

Only two participants stopped coming to the meetings. They told me when I met with them at their homes, and they let me know telling their stories was too traumatic. The mental health center offered counseling services, and I could assist with signing them up for private counseling services. Still, they asked me or their home visitors to facilitate the counseling sessions. Sadly, I shared that wasn't an option, and they left the program completely.

There is a misnomer that teen mothers have risky behavior and are "fast," especially in the black community. They actually want to be loved or are in love like the rest of us grown folks.

After the grueling 12-week sessions, it was high time for the Heart-to-Heart graduation ceremony. The Healthy Young Families team hosted the graduation ceremony at Olive Garden. We decorated the private dining room with heart-shaped balloons, tablecloths, and gift bags.

Advocacy for the Survival of Survivors

Advocacy for the survivors is important. In August 2012, I became the outreach counselor at Rape Advocacy, Counseling, and Education Services (RACES). There was a local rape crisis center, and I counseled adult survivors of child sexual abuse and adult sexual abuse. I had never thought I would be in this field, but I became an advocate for survivors, ensuring they got on the path of healing and had someone to listen to them attentively. I supported them when needed, providing them with suggestions on how to get on the right path, how to address triggers, and how they could be reintroduced to their old selves. I also let them know it's okay if you become a new person after this. And you do not have to be apologetic at all.

My counseling skills were stretched when I counseled the victims/survivors. They were sexually assaulted by men of the cloth, pediatricians, intimate partners, and international classmates. They couldn't utter anything about the abuse to anyone because cultural practice would view them as throw-away, unworthy of marriage, and shameful to their families. I never envisioned having the emotional capacity to counsel victims/survivors, and they continued with services for an average of eight months to a year. During office hours, the calls from the crisis hotline were transferred to the office.

"Rape Advocacy, Counseling, and Education Services, how may I help you."

The horrific wailing of a young black man who sounded like he was in his early 20s is what caused my vicarious trauma.

"Hello, hello, my name is Adrienne. Are you safe?"

"Yes, yes. I am not gay. I'm not."

Supportively, I said, "Okay, I believe you. You don't have to convince me. I'm here to support you." I asked again, "Are you safe?"

"I live with my aunt, and her boyfriend just got out of prison and moved in with us. When my aunt went to work, he told me to suck his dick. I said, 'NO, NO, I'm not gay.' I tried to get away from him, and he started punching me over and over again. So, I sucked it."

The caller began to cry again, much harder than before.

I sat quietly momentarily, then asked if he had a safe place to go.

Then he cleared his throat to proceed to talk with me calmly. Then, the call was disconnected.

I hopped out of my chair, entered the corridor, and asked my coworkers if there was a phone problem. Everyone checked the phones at their desks, and they worked. I summarized what had happened. None of the phones rang for about 15 minutes; when they did, it wasn't the crisis line. So many questions swirled through my head, like who is he, and did the boyfriend come home and disconnect the phone? Does he have a trusted, safe place to stay?

I would hear him wailing for two months in the middle of the night. Then I would hear my daughter crying, and then both simultaneously.

The following morning, I went to pray. I didn't recall the morning song, any testimonies, or prayer requests. The only thing I recall was rising up off my knees. At that moment, it was time to close with prayer and dismiss.

Marie spoke, "Hey, Adrienne, are you okay?"

"It's Easier to Build Strong Children Than to Repair Broken Men"- Fredrick Douglass

All I could say in between my cries was, "This young man called for help because his aunt's boyfriend sexually assaulted him, and then the call disconnected." All of a sudden, I couldn't stop crying to finish telling what had happened. Marie consoled me and proceeded to tell Apostle Smith and others what I tried to completely communicate.

Everybody laid their hands on me, and I heard Apostle Smith say clearly that day, "You don't have to carry this all by yourself. God knows your heart and love for others." Silence filled the atmosphere with soothing energy. Another closing prayer was said, and then we departed.

During my clinical supervision, I told Judy what had happened, and she said I was experiencing vicarious trauma. Vicarious trauma is the emotional residue of exposure to traumatic stories and experiences of others through work; witnessing fear, pain, and terror that others have experienced; and a preoccupation with horrific stories told to professionals.[28]

I was told to go to therapy by Judy and my executive director. The therapist basically concluded after eight sessions that black children, especially black boys, hold a special place in my heart, and I have a strong love and respect for my community. My thoughts turned to the fact that crime is associated with profit in America. The criminalization of black men and boys has been a significant cost to the community as a whole. A long time ago, my sister Dee Dee said to me that one of the saddest sights to her was seeing a black man cry. It was devastating hearing that young black man cry out for help when he most needed protection.

Maurice took me on a weekend getaway to Memphis, TN, to decompress and rejuvenate after I shared about my vicarious traumatic experience. The first night we went to King Palace to hear live blues. AutoZone was hosting a convention that week, and the place was packed. We couldn't find a seat in the house until we saw a woman sitting by herself with three empty chairs near the stage.

I kindly asked, "Are those seats taken?"

"No, y'all can sit down."

So we did with glee. We were so grateful for the seats. Maurice offered to purchase her dinner and drinks. The southern dishes started arriving: barbecue ribs, fried chicken wings, mac and cheese, and cocktails. We were breaking bread like we were cousins. Then we noticed the band leader was mouthing to the lady at the table, "Who are they?" and she smiled while chowing down on the ribs. After she sipped her drink, she let us know the band leader was her boyfriend. Maurice said, "Hell, I'll order him a drink too so we can keep our seats."

As I listened to the band, The Plantation Allstars, the music reminded me of musicians on Maxwell Street. I told Maurice and the lady, and she stated that he was from Chicago. "Damn, I have a good ear," I said. Vince, the leader of the band, came to the table and introduced himself. We all hit it off immediately. He confirmed he used to play with a band on the southeast corner on Halsted Street. Suddenly, other musicians appeared on stage, and before we knew it, we were witnessing a jam session. We danced, sang, ate, and drank until we were merry and closed the place down at 3 a.m.

The Plantation Allstars' performance reminded me of Chicago Blues Fest and Saturday morning on Maxwell Street. We attended their show throughout the weekend. Rejuvenation was an understatement, but much needed and appreciated.

Usually, I had the hotel room to myself when Maurice went on a golf outing. I did my best work in the hotels, such as completing an application for the Leadership Education, Advancement for Professional (LEAP) Fellowship, and a scholarship for Infant & Mental Health Consultant certification program at Erikson Institute. My goal with the certification was to merge infant mental health and the prevention of child sexual abuse as a new theoretical approach to adverse childhood experiences (ACEs), especially for black youth and young adults.

My first introduction to Women of Color (WOC) was when I entered the anti-gender-based-violence field. Gender-based violence is also known violence against women. First, I thought WOC was referring to black women, and it references other ethnicities of color like Mexican, Indigenous, Asian Pacific islanders (API), Middle-Eastern, members of the African diaspora, and black women whose ancestors are American descendants of slavery. Then, I had mixed emotions about the term. The LEAP Fellowship was hosted by the California Coalition Against Sexual Assault (CALCASA) and the WOC network. The fellowship was created to better prepare women of color to compete for executive roles or other administrative positions in the anti-gender-based-violence (GBV) field. Women of color were scarce in those executive roles throughout the United States and the four territories. My introduction to LEAP was at the 2013 National Sexual Assault Conference (NSAC) held in Los Angeles, CA, at Lowes Hollywood Hotel. I received a scholarship to attend. My executive director Kerri and I attended together. It was my first trip to Cali, and I thoroughly enjoyed the complementary professional development.

At NSAC, I met new friends and new peers: Carol J. Matthews-Shifflett of Utah Coalition Against Sexual Assault, Vivian Butcher St. Juste, the executive director of the Family Resource Center located in the Virgin Islands, Dr. Jonetta Neely of the Fort Wayne Police Department, and Farah Tanis, cofounder of Black Women's Blueprint. We all attended the Black Round Table discussion. It was informative and inspirational for the needs of the future of black leadership. Then, the introduction to the pilot for the LEAP Fellowship was mentioned, and it was highly encouraged for all attendees to apply if their career aspiration was to become an executive director in the anti-GBV field, such as domestic violence and sexual assault. I knew I wanted to be a decision-maker in the anti-GBV field to shift the paradigm concerning initiation, execution, and cultural leadership for the black community.

My application was third on the waitlist, but I was accepted to the 2014 pilot program. The fellowship consisted of two in-person academies, a summit, and a career coach for the duration of the one-year fellowship. The first academy was hosted in Sacramento, CA. The first person I saw and reconnected with at the hotel was Vivian. We toured Sacramento (Sac) Old Town and talked about our anticipation for the fellowship. Then, I officially met Sarah Rudolph-Pollard, who rode in the same van to the hotel. At the first academy, we all bonded, except two or three out of 20. I don't believe it was anything personal; two of the fellows didn't return for the second academy.

The coaching staff consisted of administrators from CALCASA and Women of Color Network Inc., two national anti-GBV organizations. They shared a Gaining Ground, Breaking Through study with New York University.[29] The study exposed how women of color (WOC) were not promoted to executive positions and fired without a valid reason in the feminist movement.

Also, a great number of white women didn't possess college degrees at the rate of other WOC. Women of Color were also told they didn't have enough fundraising experience so they didn't meet the qualifications to become an executive director. They interviewed WOC from multiple states that worked in domestic violence and sexual assault organizations. I was thinking, "how is it that WOC are being pushed out of a movement they helped start". Then a light bulb went off, Susan B. Anthony, Elizabeth Cady Stanton, Alice Paul, Lucy Stone, Mary Church Terrell, and Ida B. Wells were leaders of The National Woman Suffrage movement. I imagine these members of this movement were viewed as "Allies." Then on March 13, 1913, the Suffrage Parade took place in Washington, D.C. demanding women's right to vote. Interestingly, the word on the street is after Ida B. Wells established the Alpha Suffrage Club (ASC) a group of Black women from the State of Illinois to march at the parade; her and the other Black women were "told to march at the tail-end of the parade "Calmly, Ida B. Wells walked in front of the line with other Illinois delegates.

"I will cut off this right arm of mine before I will ever work or demand the ballot for the Negro and not the woman," famous quote from Susan B. Anthony.

Ironically, Black women must continue to fight for the rights to vote as opposed to other WOC. Different day, same shit! The term WOC was pushed as the new "Grand Idea."

The second academy was way better than the first. By that time, we had become better acquaintances via web conferences and grouping with assigned coaches.

The second academy was hosted in Sacramento again in the spring of 2015. Fellows had to present on issues influenced by the Violence Against Women Act (VAWA) or address challenges WOC faced trying to advance to the C-suite or a decision-making role. The VAWA reauthorization of 2013 included a solution that gave Tribal courts the authority to hold offenders in communities or reservations accountable. Which was "full of shit." It was disappointing that Native tribes had to wait until 2013 for their authority to be recognized and exercised over domestic violence defendants, whether native Indians or not. The first evening was closed out with a movie night of *Scandal* and *How to Get Away with Murder*, along with hors d'oeuvres. So, I told everyone, "Let's take some pictures." Before I left home, I had purchased a Kodak FunSaver 35mm camera since I couldn't find my digital camera. Sarah almost fell out of her chair from laughing so hard at my FunSaver.

She said, "Adrienne, where did you get that old ass camera from. It is like asking someone if they needed a ride in a 1970 Ford Pinto."

Then, we all couldn't stop laughing. We closed the second meeting with dinner and cocktails and vowed to stay in touch beyond this Fellowship. I never felt the need to pledge to a sorority because I had five biological sisters and abundant cool-ass cousins.

As the first cohort, the 15 fellows have maintained friendships and celebrated with professional collaborations and getaways, such as ATL, NC AT University homecoming, Arkansas, Las Vegas, and cabin stays in the Denver mountains.

When I flew into Chicago's O'Hare Airport from Sacramento, it was 30 below zero. The flight attendant opened the hatch to the airplane. It felt like we were outside, and Jack Frost was nipping at our noses. At that very moment, I wanted to go back to Cali.

After interviewing twice for a Mental Health Consultant position with Illinois Action for Children, I was asked to interview twice more. My former ED and the board's vice-chair encouraged me to apply for the executive director position as she would work for another statewide coalition. According to my professional circle of friends, career coach, and family, I put together a stellar presentation introducing innovative ways to diversify funding streams, become a premier organization of trauma-informed professionals and services, and establish a national collaboration as a local rape crisis center. The board and my colleagues chose someone else for the vacant ED position. I was okay with the decision, especially since the Fellowship opened my eyes to more significant opportunities aligned with my professional skills and zeal.

However, after 30 days, the new executive director terminated my employment after three years because "Illinois is an at-will state." That was not okay! Then RACES denied my unemployment, and I had to file a grievance with the state unemployment office to receive benefits four months later. This bizarre termination was a clear example that when one door closes, God will open another. My fellowship coach said, "You should consider relocating to California to work for CALCASA."

While waiting for the decision from the organization in Illinois, I went to Indianapolis with Maurice. As usual, I enjoyed the much-needed spa atmosphere. We kicked it in downtown Indy at the Jazz Kitchen and McCormick & Schmick's Seafood and Steak and danced in the hotel room. I woke up the following day to an email with a job offer for the Infant Mental Health Consultant position. I was excited to know the four interviews finally paid off. It was better to accept the job since the coalition hadn't contacted me yet.

I had a scheduled coaching call, and I was angry about the 2015 Charleston shooting, where shooter Dylan Roof killed nine black people at Emanuel African Methodist Episcopal Church after they welcomed him into the Bible study class and prayed with him. My coach said, "You should share your thoughts in a journal or with others." Before the call, I had thought this was the first time I didn't have anything to write about in the hotel. Then, I received an email inviting me to an exploratory conversation about the coalition and was scheduled for an in-person interview. Guess what, I needed to submit a writing sample and any recorded presentation before arriving at the interview. I submitted my writing sample and my lecture "Race, Gender, and the Fight to End Sexual and Structural Violence," which I had previously presented at the YWCA Friday Forum in October 2014.

My lecture opened with the history of Rosa Parks being an activist with the NAACP and an investigator and advocate for black women and girls throughout the South who were raped during the Jim Crow era. I could say that their safety was at risk, as they were domestic workers in the homes of white men, but the rape of black women and girls was a lewd American tradition, especially in the South. One of Mrs. Park's cases that made national news was the rape of a young lady named Mrs. Recy Taylor in 1944. When Mrs. Taylor was about to leave the church, a white man told her she had been identified in a crime and needed to go to the police station with him and four other men. Basically, they kidnapped her. The story ends with Mrs. Taylor being taken to the woods and raped by seven white men. One man stated he was a bystander (who the hell was he kidding!). Criminally, four white men admitted they had sex with Mrs. Taylor because she consented.

Mrs. Parks founded the Committee of Equal Justice for Mrs. Recy Taylor to bring attention to her case. This committee was supported by W. E. B. DuBois, Mary Church Terrell, and Langston Hughes, among others. The issue rose to prominence; however, the accused were never brought to justice." [30]

It wasn't until 2011, nearly 60 years after the case, that the state of Alabama formally apologized to Taylor for her treatment by the state's legal system.

In a 2011 interview, Mrs. Taylor stated, "They got me in the car and carried me straight through the woods." She said afterward they told her that if she told anyone, they would kill her.

While preparing for the talk, I became irate with the fact that white men raped black women and girls since we were kidnapped from Africa and brought to the "land of the free and the home of the brave." The 1915 movie *The Birth of a Nation* created the false narrative that black men attack innocent white women, also known as "black-on-white rape."

My lecture ended with rape culture becoming normalized and black women being unprotected. This aligned with Malcom X's quote, "The most disrespected person in America is the Black woman," in his speech to women in 1964.

Writing Sample

When we celebrate new activists such as Common, who won an Oscar for the best original song "Glory" for the movie *Selma*, there is an assumption that they understand the significance of the Jim Crow era and what the African American community endured. However, Common confidently suggested after his noted award on the Jon Stewart talk show that black Americans forget about the past and extend their hands to white people to enhance race relations. "Let's forget about the past as much as we can, and let's move from where we are now. How can we help each other? Can you try to help us because we're going to try to help ourselves, too."

Such a philosophy would have one under the impression that the United States of America is a post-racial society. As a result, when there is a denial of black people's narratives and trauma in America, it reminds me of a poignant quote by Dr. Maya Angelou: "There is no greater agony than bearing an untold story inside you."

I am agonizing over the myths about black men sexually assaulting white women, which contributed to the lynching and death of Emmett Till and others whose deaths didn't make the headlines. I am agonizing over the fact that white men raped black women and girls from slavery to the Reconstruction Era to Jim Crow, and the truth laid dormant in a society that vigorously references the U.S. Constitution and other historic documents but is not inclined to recognize the historic evidence of sexual violence against black women. I am agonizing over the fact that the domestic terrorist Dylan Roof's first statement as to why he had to kill the nine church members at Emanuel AME Church in Charleston, South Carolina, was, "You rape our women." I find that allegation quite disturbing because that belief led to centuries of black males being viewed and treated as inhuman, which has continued into the 21st century.

Dylan Roof is all of 21 years of age and quoted a statement/myth that became famous in the late 19th century. Ida B. Wells documented during her investigation of the lynching of black men that they were overwhelmingly accused of rape or attempted rape of white women. The accusation of rape was the justification and ritualization for the lynchings. I am curious how a statement of that magnitude resurfaced in a post-racial society by a young white male who was born approximately five years before the new millennium. I am agonizing over the fact that his statement was swept under the rug, and that there is no extensive dialogue about the historic fabric of the statement.

No outcry from academia, civil rights organizations, clergy, or religious sects. Unfortunately, this belief has shaped and molded a violent approach to black men. Brown men are viewed as less than human as well, so when the presidential candidate Donald Trump said, "They are, in many cases, criminals, drug dealers, rapists, etc.," that statement painted Mexican men as bestial. The Latino community challenged Trump's incorrect facts economically, politically, and socially. Consequently, he lost his business partnership with Univision and National Broadcasting

Company (NBC). On the other hand, the African American community didn't counteract the allegation Dylan Roof verbalized to the victims at Emanuel AME Church. His assertion was quoted on numerous media outlets without repair.

It is disheartening that African Americans are reluctant to stand on their platform and fall prey to anything that disdains our community.

The interview with CALCASA took place in October 2015 in Sacramento at the Coalition for a Training and Technical Assistance position while I was waiting for the next steps of the grievance process for my previous position at RACES. I was getting dressed at the Marriott Residence Hotel for the interview. Then, the news stated two outside experts had concluded a Cleveland police officer's fatal shooting of Tamir Rice was a reasonable response as he was perceived as a threat. My friend Shandra happened to call me to wish me well for the interview. I was bawling and wailing, and I couldn't collect myself. My eyes were puffy and red as red Kool-Aid. The therapist's diagnosis of my vicarious trauma entered my many emotions: "Black children, especially black boys, hold a special place in your heart, and you have a strong love and respect for your community."

We talked for five more minutes and ended the call with prayer. Thank God I wore glasses that hid the distinct look of my eyes that could've been mistaken for a DUI gaze.

The wait to hear from unemployment and the Coalition grew exhausting. So, I went and stayed at DeeDee's house in Chicago. I spent time with my parents and took them to several doctors' appointments. Then, I received the call with a job offer in November. First, I was indecisive because I wanted to leverage the offer from IL Action For Children and CALCASA. I was quite confident an offer was coming, but not so late. So, I accepted the job offer to be an infant mental health consultant since CALCASA still hadn't contacted me 30 days after the interview.

I officially accepted the offer on December 4th and relocated to Sacramento on January 4th, 2016. I was starting this new adventure across the country without my children. I also ended that chapter with my "means of escape," Maurice. This was my first time residing in a state where I only knew two people: my fellowship coach and my new executive director.

CHAPTER XIV

"BLESSED SHALT THOU BE IN THE CITY, AND BLESSED SHALT THOU BE IN THE FIELD" (DEUTERONOMY 28:3-5, KJV)

When I reached Sacramento, my goal was to grow professionally and spiritually. I climbed the career ladder by becoming a staff member of CALCASA, a national organization. The office was on the 18th floor, overlooking the state capitol and downtown restaurants. The organization provides training, technical assistance, and policy advocacy for rape crisis centers and domestic violence organizations throughout California.

We hosted national conferences bi-annually for about 2,100 anti-GBV professionals and statewide meetings for 500 California professionals.

I grew fond of Sacramento, also known as Sac Town, Capital City, and River City. Let me be clear, it was no Chicago, but it had some great attributes, such as a strong activism platform and strong interfaith community. My favorite Sac Town nonprofit organizations were led by people who look liked the populations they served and represented, such as Voices Of The Youth founder and executive director Berry Accius, Women of Color on the Move founder and CEO Sonia Pellerin, My Sister's House executive director Nilda Guanzon Valmores, and Underground Books founder Kevin Johnson, former NBA player and former mayor of Sacramento. His mother Georgia "Mother Rose" West manages the store. Underground Books was brought into existence in 2003, when the only library in the Oak Park community had been shut down in the 1970s. It became a literacy hub and a place for community members to have access to books.

One Saturday, the author Maria P. Herndon introduced herself and talked briefly about her early years of teaching math at Lindblom High School, located on the South Side of Chicago. Our eyes met automatically after "South Side of Chicago"—an instant connection and a gleam of admiration appeared upon our faces. Then, she read excerpts from her book, *A Man to Love: Finding Love When You Have Long Given Up*. While Ms. Maria was vocalizing the words off the pages, I envisioned and felt as if she was saying black love is a love comparable to the African proverb "Let your love be like the misty rain, coming softly but flooding the river." The plot cheered for black love among two emotionally damaged African American professionals. Before the afternoon was over, Ms. Maria invited me to visit her church, First Baptist Church in Sacramento.

Eventually, I was led to visit First Baptist Church with Pastor Lamar J. Pringle for approximately four months. After the service, we had lunch and some of the best discussions about family and our grandchildren. Maria said that I should attend the women's Bible study series, the Whole Armor of God. I used to quote Ephesians 6:11, I'm gonna *"put on the whole armor of God"* to get me through my hard days. I attended Priscilla Shirer's "Whole Armor of God" seven-session Bible study via video, hosted by Charlie Darrington, Minister of Women's Ministers for Women's ministry. This transformative study led me to gain new spiritual insights and expand my understanding of prayer. Sessions two and three spoke to my spirit: "The Belt of Truth" and "The Breastplate of Righteousness." The belt of truth is the core support when you're in a spiritual war. And the Roman soldiers wore breastplates to protect their upper bodies, especially their hearts. The biblical metaphor is "the difference between life and death." What the breastplate did for the Roman soldier's physical heart, righteousness does for your spiritual heart.

It was 2016, eleven years after the trauma, and homicide was still in my purview. My heartfelt heartbreak was more on some days than on others. For seven weeks, seven women attended the class consistently. We enjoyed the dialogue and each other's company so much we were invited to another church women's ministry movie night. The featured film was *War Room*, with Priscilla Shirer as the main character. The church was decorated like the movie, with all theater snacks, hot dogs, popcorn, and gobblers, except with some gospel music in the background. We had so much fun, as black folks do. We talked and laughed during the movie. It felt like a movie in downtown Chicago. Some of the chit-chat was about the husband, Tony's, cold and callous tone, and he was considering an extramarital affair with a colleague. Yes, we were in church, but the moviegoers sounded like they were ready to "knuck if you buck (swing if you hard or if you want to fight, then let's do it.)." The night ended with a raffle and prayer. I won a prayer wall bulletin board set. The prize was needed more than ever before since I didn't have an official prayer group yet, my means of survival.

Another day at the office, my sister DD, also known as Janie, called me to share some unsettling news about a young teenager, Marcie Gerald, who attended junior high with my nephew, Jordan. I then shared the story with my colleague Tiffany, who later became my colleague-friend after she came to assist me one morning with some technical challenges on my Mac. She always forewarned me to hide or close some of the numerous tabs opened on my laptop before she came over. It drove her crazy. We were talking about work and social justice. Then, all of a sudden, I grabbed the back of my thigh and started sliding off of my chair onto the floor. I couldn't say one word, only mouthed. "Oh my God! God, God!"

"Are you having a heart attack?" she screamed. Then Tiffany ran from the front of the cubicle.

"I caught a charley horse," I muttered.

To this day, I don't know how that term came about, but I know what it meant. She started massaging the front and back of my right thigh. Afterward, I "came back," like from a heart attack.

"Girl, I thought you were having a cardiac arrest."

"Sorry, I started the new rowing machine at 24-hour fitness, and obviously, I wasn't fit enough to be rowing on that damn machine."

Tiffany became my first colleague-friend in Cali that day.

The Apology

The mother of Marcie Gerald, Elizabeth, wrote an article in *The Reporters Inc.* calling on the black community and church to address suicide, sexual assault, and mental health. I read the article and was so saddened by the fact that this young lady had her whole life ahead of her and it was taken away by suicide the day her rapist was released from the county jail for another crime he had committed.

I was inspired to write this blog. As a black woman who works in the sexual violence field, I feel the need to apologize to Marcie Gerald for failing to expand the conversation around the intersectionality of trauma and mental health. Apologetically, I sympathize with her mom, Elizabeth Gerald's, grieving and mourning for the loss of Marcie's innocence and promise. I kept the conversation at work and within my circle of trust. I came to realize the phrase "What happens/is said in this house stays in this house" is like an African American proverb. When we accept such a statement, it becomes a tradition and increases the secrecy and silence of the issues pertaining to the black community, particularly women. Understandably, families prefer to work on solutions among themselves and determine when and to whom to reveal the information. On the other hand, secrecy doesn't allow details to be brought to light by anyone. Black girls'/women's trauma and mental health have always been silenced from slavery to the Reconstruction Era to Jim Crow and now this millennium. The trauma that black women had and continue to endure is still hidden in darkness and remains a mystery within and outside the black community. We must enlighten the masses that the marginalization of black girls and women is a historical fabric in our society and perpetrated by our own community. We can no longer accept it.

Sixty percent of black girls have experienced sexual abuse at the hands of black men before reaching the age of 18, according to a study conducted by Black Women's Blueprint. As a community, we are quite boisterous about the potential trauma some black men may face for the abusive behaviors they exhibit (e.g., R. Kelly) because the black community has this sense of protectionism for the black man. Black women and girls are not protected and rescued in the same manner. There is a distorted notion that black women are strong and capable of handling any obstacle that comes their way because our foremothers had to do it and taught their lineage coping mechanisms to survive. Unfortunately, that survival mechanism has been mistaken for bionic strength and has dehumanized black women. So, that misguided thought was the pathway for our victimization, criminalization and ostracization. This isolation adds another layer to the stigma and silence, which hinders the much-needed conversation about therapeutic approaches and responses.

I concur with Mrs. Gerald that the black community is "the most religious race," so I highly suggest we transition some of the religious belief and dedication to address the trauma and mental health that's embedded in our community, families and institutions.

First, we can start this movement by sharing Marcie Gerald's story and supporting Mrs. Gerald's legislative mission. Second, let's utilize mental health services that are responsive to communities of color, specifically African Americans. If cultural and spiritual specific services are not available in our communities, we need to advocate for the service delivery and funding. In contrast, astronomical funding is allocated to the criminal justice system to serve black men, so we can and must demand the same. Third, amplify conversations along with public awareness/campaigns about adverse childhood experiences, their connection to trauma and long-term health and social consequences, and their impact on the black community. The normalization of signs and symptoms of traumatic stress and mental health can help with de-stigmatization. Lastly, the empowerment for black girls and women is detrimental for their mental health.

Most importantly, it will afford them the opportunity to become the promise that's within them.

Immediately after I read the heart-wrenching article, I shared the blog post with my current director at the time, and she stated "We're not ready for this blog, "it seems too personal. The response took me aback because it was in the organization's purview. I said, "Oh, okay." The purpose of the blog was to initiate the conversation about the impact of child sexual assault, especially on black girls, and the needed support from the black community and church.

Approximately two weeks later, my director called me and said, "Why don't you do some mapping for faith-led organizations that are addressing sexual assault or are willing to?" At once, I started googling faith-based organizations addressing sexual assault and prevention of child sexual abuse. There were slim pickings for what I was really hoping to come across, for example, a curriculum and training. Honestly, I was puzzled and uncertain of what I really wanted to come of this new project, especially since it was fragile and overexposed by a particular religious sect. A few work hours per day were allotted to researching anything about faith-based organizations and sexual assault.

My research continued throughout the weekends, reviewing scholarly abstracts about faith organizations addressing sexual violence. However, they were related to HIV/AIDS on the continent of Africa and trauma, but not specifically sexual assault. Interestingly, some multi-faiths recognized October as Domestic Violence (DV) Awareness Month, but not Sexual Assault Awareness Month (SAAM). It was brought to my attention that DV is easier to frame as a family matter potentially caused by stress. On the other hand, sexual assault is plagued with stigmas and stereotypes such as that rape, molestation, and sexual assault are rare, or they only happen to a certain type of person, and if a person didn't verbally say no, it doesn't count as rape.

The research was becoming tedious and discombobulated. A much-needed break was in order. So, I had to attend the second FORCE Upsetting Rape Culture Leadership Team retreat in Blue Mountain Center in Blue Mountain Lake, NY. FORCE is an amazing art-activist organization founded by Rebecca Nagle and Hannah Brancato. The two Baltimore feminists became famous after they spoofed Victoria Secret by adding "No Means No" on their panties and sharing it on social media. It was such a hit that many people thought Victoria Secret had a new conscience campaign. The purpose of the retreat was to plan for the blanketing of the National Mall in June 2019 with the Monument Quilt, a collection of over 3,000 stories by survivors of sexual and intimate partner violence and allies, written, painted, and stitched onto red fabric.

FORCE was an intersectional, LGBTQ-focused, multicultural, inter-faith, pro-black, and anti-white supremacist collective that did their deepest organizing work in Baltimore and Mexico City and planted seeds globally. Twenty-six members of the leadership team that arrived in New York came from as far as California, North Carolina, Illinois, North Dakota, Maryland, and Mexico. The first day, we hung out at the lake where some swam in the two lakes that adjoined. I sang some Sam Cooke and Motown hits safely on the dock of the bay with JP. We harmonized pretty darn well since we didn't rehearse. When we all got together, it was always like a homecoming party, with us happy to see each other. And the reunions were never without an emphasis on radical advocacy.

Then, I met a new member of the leadership team, and we shared the personal and professional projects we were working on. They told me they were a Fellow with the Just Beginning Collaborative. They suggested I contact another Fellow, Linda Crockette, at Samaritan Safe Church, who wrote a curriculum that offers training to faith organizations to prevent child sexual abuse. I said I came across Linda during my mapping, and she was on my contact list. Linda and I developed a successful partnership and friendship after we met.

Linda and my workshop proposal to present at the California Partnership to End Domestic Violence (CPEDV) 2016 Statewide Conference, "Faith-based and Anti-Gender-Based Violence Organizations Partner to Approach Healing Prevention," was accepted. Linda and I worked tirelessly over the telephone and via email to assemble the presentation. We finally met in person at a networking reception in San Diego the night before our presentation. It was hilarious when we met face-to-face because all we could do was laugh and hug each other. We were so adamant about and dedicated to the work around preventing child sexual abuse. She flew from Lancaster, PA, to San Diego, a three-hour time zone difference, to bring awareness and advocate for cross-movement collaboration between the faith community and the anti-gender-based violence field. I felt like this long-distance relationship was finally coming together. It felt as if God had invited me to partner with Him specifically for this project. Remember, I wasn't recruited to do faith-based work. As a non-offending parent, it was an indirect way of soothing my anger.

The drum roll started at 10 a.m. The session was filled to capacity with professionals from all levels in the anti-GBV field and other state agencies. A couple of faith leaders were in the audience. Peter Celum was an executive director at Lassen Family Services in Susanville, CA, that also offered therapy to victimized children of child sexual abuse in rural areas, and he was also a clergy member. There were more nonbelievers of what the church could offer to help end child sexual abuse than those trying to

"Blessed Shalt Thou Be in the City, and Blessed Shalt Thou Be in the Field" (Deuteronomy 28:3-5, KJV)

get atheists to convert. I understood the skepticism because the headlines were filled with churches and child sexual abuse cases throughout the U.S. and internationally, such as "Priest and church leaders sexually abused hundreds of children in Altoona Diocese" (AG Office) and "The Theft of Innocence: Voluntourism and Child Sexual Abuse" (Media Diversified). On the other hand, some people were open to the presentation and the upcoming three-day training for faith leaders and staff on domestic violence and sexual assault. At the end of the presentation, Peter came up to the podium to introduce himself to me and Linda. Then, the making of history began.

That night, Linda and I had dinner with three fabulous women: Karen, Debra, and Dana, executives at a domestic violence organization in LA called Jenesse Center, Inc. We talked about the impact of domestic violence on families and how faith organizations could be integral in providing support to families and partnering with domestic violence organizations. Let's say the evening was a cross between a women's leadership forum and heads tilted back with the laughter of old acquaintances. I told them about when I had my first-ever allergic reaction to shrimp at the age of 36. My sister Dee Dee surprised me with a trip to St. Andrews, Scotland, and Killarney, Ireland. She won a marketing award from her employer and an all-expenses-paid trip, and she invited me to go with her. A few days before departure, my features resembled Quasimodo, aka the Hunchback of Notre Dame.

FaceTime wasn't as popular then. Dee Dee said, "Girl, it can't be that bad. I will see you at O'Hare Airport." We met face-to-face without any laughter or hugs. I greeted her with," Hey, girl," and her eyes resembled a deer encountering headlights, and her body jerked suddenly as someone touched her unexpectedly from behind. "Oh, hey, girl," she muddled. "It doesn't look that bad!" she exclaimed. Of all the places to visit, I had to go to Europe, where the story of the Hunchback of Notre Dame began.

In 2018, I attended the California Partnership to End Domestic Violence (CPEDV) Statewide Conference in San Francisco. I had the pleasure of seeing the executive team again. They invited my colleague Kristelyn and me to present our conference workshop, "The Missing Middle: Black Women Leadership and Changing the Paradigm," to the administrative team at their organization since they could not attend our workshop.

Colleague-Friends in the Pasadena Office

It was October 2017, and I was invited to work in the Pasadena office, where the intervention and advocacy team would be housed. I attended an "A Call to Men" event in LA and a meeting at the Pasadena office. The staff consisted of Imelda, the sophisticated Filipino debutante, Liliana, the fashionista, and Elizabeth, the precious little sister of the Pasadena office. Elizabeth's nickname, "little sister," was so befitting, especially when Imelda and I expressed excitement that Janet Jackson was going to be in concert. Our little sister asked, "Did she make some good songs?" Imelda and I gasped and realized we were Gen Xers and officially the elders of the Millennials. During the meeting, I was also promoted to program coordinator. At that very moment, the colleague-friendship was forged. Imelda and I worked on the LEAP Program and other advocacy projects together. Elizabeth was the program assistant, and Liliana was the project coordinator for the Prison Rape Elimination Act (PREA) statewide program. The office was a space with an ambiance of creativity and energy awaiting innovation and emerging challenges in the sexual assault field. The office was located in Old Town Pasadena, where popular retail stores and restaurants were in abundance, such as Tiffany & Co. Jewelry Store, Crate & Barrel, J. Crew, Fleming's Prime Steakhouse & Wine Bar, Yard House, and Starbucks. Our lunch breaks and after-work happy hour were a script of shits and giggles, taking selfies and enjoying noonday cocktails from Starbucks.

We discussed every subject from childhood memories and platonic and intimate relationships to politics, especially the 2016 presidential election. The restaurant was full of right-wing supporters and people enthusiastic to claim their well-deserved victory. The night of the election, we went to the Yard House for happy hour and watched the election coverage. My intense observation of the TV screen was starting to resemble my unconscious thoughts that Hillary "Hill" Clinton wouldn't be the winner to select the next booty for the SCOTUS seat that the outgoing POTUS didn't appoint. The blue donkey's campaign was not as shrewd as the red elephants, and their strategies were too innocent, like doves. The poll numbers were shrinking as fast as corporations' tax responsibilities. The night closed with depressed looks, tears, and "I can't believe it." We were also thinking about what the hell was going to happen, since the "pussy grabber" was the new POTUS and would overlook the Office on Violence Against Women (OVW) and the Violence Against Women Act (VAWA).

A Women's March was planned for March 2017 to protest against Trump's election. My former director shared that the agency was supporting the march and that we all needed to

"Blessed Shalt Thou Be in the City, and Blessed Shalt Thou Be in the Field" (Deuteronomy 28:3-5, KJV)

come together. My response was, "I envisioned this march would resemble the Women's Suffrage March, where black women were told to march from behind after the tireless coalition building. I won't be joining this bandwagon." She looked at me as if she was clutching her pearls. Ironically, my friend Brittany and I discussed at great length during Pacific and Eastern Time zones how the march had politically co-opted the messages of two historical moments in black history, The Million Women March led by Black Women in 1997 and the March on Washington, where Dr. Martin Luther King Jr. delivered his "I Have a Dream" speech in 1963. The pink pussyhats and pink vagina costumes didn't scream solidarity to me at all.

Then, three more kick-ass professional women were added to the office: Kristelyn, Julianna, and Terri. This crew was divinely structured; we fed off each other professionally and personally. Kristelyn, the brilliant black southern belle from Norfolk, VA; Terri, the attorney of law who graced the nonprofit sector with her esquire exquisiteness; and Julianna, the seasoned woman who exhibited all the qualities of a Quinceanera. Our temperaments were quite different but compatible, and we had a bond similar to the characters of the movie *Set It Off*, minus robbing banks. We celebrated each other's wins, dreams, birthdays, and holidays. We celebrated birthdays in and out of the office with a big shebang, cakes from a bakery in Old Pasadena, catered food, homemade entrees, decorations, selfies, and laughter.

Being in each other's company was so genuine and enjoyable. During our many amusing dialogues, I shared about a pact my sister Dee Dee and I made some years ago. We vowed that if one of us were ever in a coma, we would comb each other's hair, pluck

"Blessed Shalt Thou Be in the City, and Blessed Shalt Thou Be in the Field" (Deuteronomy 28:3-5, KJV)

unruly chin hairs, wax hairs above the lip before they became a full-blown mustache, and clip and polish each other toenails. We were no longer just sisters; we became "coma friends." Then, the offer was extended to these amazing colleagues because I had no family on the West Coast. They were all game, except when I explained the importance of cosmetic treatment for my toenails and feet. Kristelyn quick-wittedly said, "I will tweeze your chin hairs, but I'm not going near your feet!" Generously, Julianna promised to polish my toenails with a chuckle. They were willing to extend our friendship as my SoCal "coma friends," but with limits.

As a result, my colleague-friends were concerned about my returning home since I didn't have any family in SoCal, let alone in California. So, they offered to pay for membership to eHarmony, the online dating service. I reassured them a man wasn't the reason I relocated and wouldn't be the reason I would leave. But I accepted their offer. Immediately, I connected with a black guy, Lawrence, who worked in the aerospace field. He lived about 30 minutes west of the Topanga Village. We both listed our R&B and singing group LTD as an admired group. His previous matches were white women, and he was surprised to be matched with a black woman from the East Coast. "Geographically, there is a massive chunk of land East of California before you officially arise on the East Coast, called the Midwest," I exclaimed.

We talked on the phone for about two weeks before our first date. He initiated a discussion about where we had traveled domestically and internationally. The conversation was cut short as I shared the many states and countries I had had the opportunity to visit. Ground rules were set, and we would meet halfway,

"Blessed Shalt Thou Be in the City, and Blessed Shalt Thou Be in the Field" (Deuteronomy 28:3-5, KJV)

approximately 45 minutes to the destination. Of course, I got input from my "Set It Off" crew. I would arrive at the location and take a photo of his license plates and a photo of his driver's license and forward it to a group text for safety purposes. I shared the plan with him, and he said, "I want you to know that if I don't show up to work without notification, the authorities will kick in my apartment door for safety purposes." "What, Negro?" I said in my head. So, safety was a shared concern for both of us.

"My friends are sophisticated and are most capable of kicking in doors with authority," I added. Mr. aerospace man was a veteran with some supposed government clearance. Before he ended the call, he said, "I will be wearing some docker khaki pants, a polo shirt, and no flip flops." I said, "Okay. Good night."

We met at one of my favorite restaurants, Maggiano's Little Italy. I wore a strapless jumpsuit, and my hair was flat ironed and flowing like a feather from a swan. Embarrassingly, I tried to enter the wrong door to the restaurant when arriving 15 minutes late. He watched me when I exited my car and entered the restaurant. He was dressed just as he had informed me. All he needed was a blazer to look like he would approve a bank loan for me. He greeted me with a big box of See's Candies. We sat in a big booth across from each other. I realized he spoke soft and low. I offered to sit next to him to hear him better and engage in the conversation. At first, I didn't know what the hell he was saying. Before we departed, he walked me to my car, and I took pictures of his license plate and ID to send to my friends. He asked if he could kiss me. I assured him I would not kiss on the first date, but he could kiss my cheek, which he obliged. Then I told him that since he had the pleasure of kissing the right dimple he was welcome to kiss the left dimple. He did and thanked me profusely before he laughed and said, "You are funny." Parting was such sweet sorrow because the date was entertaining, and I thought about the next time we would see each other. It was a nice date since my last first date had been in 2005.

Afterward, we went on several dates, for instance, to the Getty Museum, Johnny Rockets restaurants, and to the movies to see *Detroit*. I also trained for the 2018 LA Marathon with the World Vision Religion Organization. Every time we met, he purchased so much produce from the farmers markets for me that I had to take it to work on Monday to share with my office mates.

Lawrence also offered me free massages through the credits he earned at the company Massage Envy because he was a dedicated member. I thoroughly enjoyed the free weekly massages. All he asked was that I give the masseuse a nice tip. Massage tips were a part of my line-item budget. Soon after, we met at the movies at the Glendale Galleria Movie Theater to see *Girls Trip*. My colleagues questioned whether we should watch that kind of movie since we hadn't been dating for a long time. "Hell, we're grown," I giggled. At first, he tried to be as conservative as his outfit on our first date. It took him a moment to lighten up. Then we laughed so hard, notably when Jada Pinkett was ziplining from one hotel to another and peed on the crowd below in the French Quarter.

The vibe began changing gradually. Out of nowhere, he told me it was unusual for him to drive such a distance for a date on a weekday. "I can't believe how nice you are," he expressed. In my mind, I wondered who he had previously dated. "Mommy Dearest (Mommy Dearest is a 1981 movie based on actress

"Blessed Shalt Thou Be in the City, and Blessed Shalt Thou Be in the Field" (Deuteronomy 28:3-5, KJV)

Joan Crawford, who is portrayed as abusive, controlling, and manipulative adoptive mother.)," I asked how he would like to proceed with this dating setup.

Later, he suggested we be friends since he was applying for jobs outside California. I wholeheartedly supported that proposal, but he continued to call at least two to three times a week. I reminded him of his recommendation.

"I like talking to you," he said.

I told him, "You are treating me like a fat girl."

Do you know how fat girls are considered pleasant and willing to be friends? At the same time, engaging in a platonic relationship requires emotional, psychological, and therapeutic capital. I promised Lawrence I wouldn't be a "fat girl" in need of a superficial, intimate relationship. On the other hand, I was willing to be the "fat girl" for the weekly massages for a tip, not the actual cost of the massage, but I didn't let Lawrence know that part. He started to work my nerves with wishy-washy behavior and continued his calls, but I couldn't wean myself from the free massages, so I continued to answer his calls. I wanted to blame my colleagues for the situation. I felt like a member of Alcoholic Anonymous: I am an alcoholic but sneaking a drink with guilt. The day came when I was ready to fess up and take full responsibility. The day of my last free massage was like breaking off a committed relationship without closure. The masseuse was phenomenal, with magnetic fingers and palms. I woke up, thanked her profusely, and gave her an additional $10 tip. While walking to my car, I hit a block on my cell phone. The following Monday, I told the office crew what had happened and said, "It is what it is."

That afternoon, it was communicated that celebrations were no longer welcomed and effective immediately, bringing it to a halt! When I started working at that office, the administrator hosted and invited staff to the in-office gathering. We said, "Whatever, a new policy will not stop us from practicing our celebratory moments outside the office."

Shockingly, three of my colleagues/friends were fired a week later, just like employees at the U.S. Postal System. "Going postal" wasn't their response to the unexpected gruff treatment from the administrative staff that fired them due to "budgetary constraints" (meme face). The way they were escorted out of the office was more criminal than Bernie Madoff (largest Ponzi scheme, $64.8 billion) and Jeffrey Keith Skilling (Enron Scandal). I didn't have access to or authority over the agency's budget, but it's not what you do, it's how you do it. My friends' class and graciousness filled the spiritless atmosphere throughout the ordeal.

After that fiasco, we went on a friendcation to Big Bear for the weekend. We expressed our disappointment with how a nonprofit anti-gender-based-violence organization led by WOC's latest practice strongly resembled white supremacy and patriarchy, the system and structure they wanted to dismantle. As usual, our time together began with fun canoeing, cooking meals, hanging out in the village, and taking group photos and selfies. We fed off each other's energy in the most rewarding way. Our friendship remains six years after the unexpected and disheartening encounter with people who thought of themselves as "disruptive leaders." One of the leaders' proverbial statements was, "Every sister ain't your sista."

CHAPTER XV

PROJECT FATE

The Samaritan Safe Church mobilized a national, multi-denominational, faith-based movement to end child sexual abuse. CALCASA hosted the first train-the-trainer session at First Baptist Church in Sacramento. The Samaritan Safe Church training was successful, with twelve attendees from Susanville, Napa Valley, Stockton, and Roseville. The three-day sessions were filled with tears, amens, and holding onto the prayers of God's promises to all who believed and inquired about His unwavering grace. Stories from the Bible enlightened the curriculum by sharing the sexual assault of David's daughter, Tamar, by her brother, Amon. In all my life of attending church and listening to sermons, I have never heard of the story of Tamar or her name except on the *Braxton Family Values* reality show. Sadly, Tamar's treatment and her victimization ushered a tradition to today's response to sexual assault. She had to advocate for herself indirectly by wearing sackcloth to indicate that she had experienced a problem without identifying the perpetrator or any accountability.

Tamar's abuse took place in her home, the same as my daughter's, and both fathers played a role in the abuse directly and indirectly without any responsibility for their daughters' safety.

The closing session ended with the benediction to forgive or not to forgive. In Matthew 18:21-22, Jesus told St. Peter to forgive his brother's sin against him seventy times seven. According to some commentary, forgiveness should be limitless. Many Christians would hold onto that scripture for dear life, even if the one who sinned against them didn't ask for forgiveness. The intense curriculum ensued disclosure of personal experiences and holding in guilt for not wanting to forgive the abuser who abused them and younger family members. I was still wrestling with the conscience to kill, and the thought of forgiveness was like trying to put out a grease fire with water. "Come on, God, help me. You want me to forgive Jeff after all he has done?"

Subconsciously, I was trying to bargain with God. I felt forgiving would dismiss Jeff's brutal acts and his accountability. Forgiveness is a form of denial, I insisted. The forgiveness circle ended with "What do we mean by forgiveness?" and "Is forgiveness one size fits all?" It is up to the individual to decide their path to forgiveness.

For the closing activity, everyone stood in a circle to discuss how they felt about the curriculum on forgiveness. Now, most attendees were believers who worked in the anti-gender-based-violence field or ministry. The curriculum was aligned with the biblical text. However, the facial expressions looked puzzled or unsettled, as if they were in Las Vegas at the craps tables. Should I bet, or shouldn't I bet again?

St. Peter was known for his rash responses and faith; he walked on water when Jesus commanded him to (Matthew 14:28). If I had to face St. Peter at the gates of heaven at this very moment, I'd say "You were the one who cut off the ear of the high priest's servants arresting Jesus" (John 18:10), and "You used profanity; you were the disciple with the characteristics of a soldier protecting your master. Don't start; none won't be none. I shall not tell a lie," according to Leviticus 19:11. Indeed, St. Peter would understand my stance because I was of faith, and my rashness was driven to protect. He also had many bouts and came around in due time.

I don't believe victims/survivors are obligated to forgive. My unhealed heart was reasoning with the holy spirit. I was using scripture to justify my unwillingness to forgive. Well, Lawd, I'm not at the forgiving stage yet. Sadly, I was speaking from my anger and hurt.

After the training, Peter Celum, the executive director of Lassen Family Services and a minister, accepted the offer to host an eight-month cohort of seven churches in Susanville, CA. I had the spiritual pleasure of providing technical assistance to Peter and the group, and Linda's organization funded the project. Despite the climate of child sexual abuse among denominational churches, I felt the church still had some validity and safe churches could exist.

The Samaritan Safe Church Cohort consisted of seven churches in Susanville, CA. They met one Saturday a month for eight months. Since I was the technical assistant for the project, I facilitated one session for the cohort. Due to a conflict, I rescheduled my session to lead, and unbeknownst to me, the lesson plan for that Saturday was "The Grooming Process: What Every Adult Needs to Know about Child Sexual Abuse and Incest, the Grooming Process, and Non-offending Parents." I wasn't sure if I was ready. Would my unresolved anger protrude into my voice and my facial expression, or would I scream from the top of my lungs? I'd never told my whole story. The session was like a communal conversation among puzzled parents wanting to ensure they never earned the title of non-offending. Sharing my story was therapeutic because it's not a subject matter to initiate a discussion or introduction: "Hello, my name is Adrienne, and I'm a non-offending parent." But this was the perfect place for me to make such an introduction. Some attendees were pastors for youth, women, married, and counseling ministries that wanted to utilize the knowledge to equip the churches better to support congregates and the community.

Also, they wanted to help shape policies within the church. Initially, the class met for three hours, and this session lasted 40 minutes longer. First, the non-offending parent was new to everyone except the child's sexual therapist. The dialogue was enriched with questions on how offenders gain the child's and parents' trust before sexually exploiting the child. Most importantly, support is needed for the non-offending parent. It felt like I was back at RACES, counseling victims/survivors throughout the training, but this time the trauma-informed approach was for me. I had to recall the strength-based approach it took for me to be available to my children. Throughout this experience, I have been inspired to understand better and address the impact of trauma on mothers of children who have been abused. I was invited to be a keynote speaker at the Community Church of Susanville's Empower Conference in October 2018.

The title of my speech was "Project Fate." The primary purpose was to introduce myself as a non-offending parent (NOP) and ask the faith community to take the lead in supporting this community of parents. After defining NOP, I displayed the artistic mask I made for the art displayed for survivors of sexual abuse. The mask had brown and bronze skin, closed eyes with a gold crown, a rope draped over the face looking through a cage, and a head with multiple green feathers outlining the top. The title was," I Was So Green I Was Blinded By the Truth." I also shared some of the most detrimental effects of child sexual abuse: the relationship between the abused child and the non-offending parent is often compromised when enhanced intra-familiar support is most needed, such as through rage and broken faith. But God showed me the importance of wearing God's whole armor as a way to heal.

I was on the trajectory of accomplishing these feats with my dual membership at Friendship Pasadena Church and Pasadena Church, being a part of Team World Vision, a Christian organization training for the 2018 LA Marathon, We Can Stop STDs LA (Interfaith Committee), Fuller Theological Seminary's WOC bag lunch group, Greater Pasadena Affordable Housing Group (GPAHG) faith-based housing justice, two Bible study groups, a prayer group, and attending the Clergy Coalition monthly meetings.

God's embrace was comforting my outward and inward tears throughout this journey. I believe my relocation to California was God's way of lowering me down in front of all the spiritual people who would guide me in the last leg of my healing journey and evaluate my faith, as in Luke 5:17-39, where a disabled man's friends lowered him down to Jesus through a hole in the roof for healing.

Over the years, I've overcompensated for my pain by staying busy. The difference this time was that I was spiritually productive, and that was accompanied with spiritual insight. I closed with an all-call to the faith community to invest in a ministry to acknowledge and support non-offending parents. I don't believe Jesus wants us to carry this cross of abuse ourselves. Additionally, believe it or not, the faith community is a trendsetter. We're still quoting scripture from before the Birth of Christ (BC) and paying tithes.

Once I finished, a long line formed in the lobby, waiting to speak with me. I listened and talked to every parent in line. They all had similar sentiments: "Thank you. Nobody ever talks about non-offending parents or recognizes us as the other victims trying to get through the pain." Through my pleading voice, I said that there will be times when trying to make meaning of it all can be overwhelming. You have the right to remember and address it; if you don't, your body will.

On Sunday afternoon, the congregations of the seven churches received community training to get a general overview of the curriculum with a focus on child safety in the church or just recognition of some trauma about child sexual abuse. We also provided education and policy training regarding various forms of abuse. Peter, Linda, and I facilitated the congregational training for about 90 people. The training was engaging and well-received. One of the pastors in the cohort had expressed her skepticism when invited to join. She stood up in the sanctuary to give testimony about how learning about the grooming process helped her assist with saving some young ladies from being preyed on by an adult in a chaperone position. I then stressed that preventing child sexual abuse is strength-based and not just doom and gloom; for example, it involves teaching children as young as toddlerhood to communicate effectively and know what makes them feel comfortable and safe. This is a great time to start drafting or redrafting how you will implement protective factors to help build a strong family—being the first teacher to your children and teaching them to communicate their emotions and to have strong social connections. We closed with me sharing a training I put together for a support group for adult survivors of adult and child sexual abuse.

The gist was that they did not have to conform to the tradition of foreplay and pillow talk. I was on stage about 10 feet from the audience, and they looked shocked and astounded. I wasn't going to orate the story as a harlot as some may have imagined. I wasn't dismissive of their wariness and uncertainty about my following words. The support group survivors exhibited similar expressions, and others were more baffled.

I'm not a traditional young lady; nor are my intimate preferences. Every week, my ex-boyfriend would supply me with a list of NCAA and NFL football teams competing to win. No money was involved, only pride. I know what God said about pride in Psalm 75:4: *"I say to the boastful, 'Do not boast.'"* Okay, I'm guilty as charged. Luckily for him, the payout wasn't money, just a little gloating. That interaction was arousing. I looked him in the eye and said, "Stick with me, and you will always win, smooches."

The audience roared with laughter, and some men shook their heads, probably thinking my opportunity to gloat was sheer luck. By this time, they were open to the example of pillow talk. I said survivors should exercise their power and control and reconfigure what and how it will make them feel safer and more secure. And for me, engaging in conversations about the political climate or current events made for great pillow talk. This is how to support survivors' attempts to liberate themselves from the chains of past abuse and walk with them on their path to healing. On my way home, I had to apologize to God for asking him to help me with revenge. Then, I thanked God for showing me I was not my trauma.

Statements of Gratitude

In closing, Psalm 40:9-10 (ESV) is the best way to express my sincere gratitude.

It was Wednesday, April 19, 2019, at the 7 p.m. Bible study at Friendship Pasadena Church in Pasadena, California. After the Bible study class, Pastor Lucious W. Smith sang a hymn and asked if anyone had a testimony or anything to share. I raised my hand and stated I had called my ex-husband on Sunday to express my sincere condolences for the loss of his mother. We talked for about 45 minutes to an hour. I realized I was finally in a place of healing and forgiveness because, once upon a time, I had contemplated how to kill him and make a homicide look like a suicide.

Sister Charlotte Bailey said, "Did you say …?" and before she could complete her question, Pastor Smith said, "Yes, she said homicide into a suicide."

To think it took me from January 2005 until April 19, 2019, to admit the heinous thoughts I once harbored publicly. I needed peace, and the Prince of Peace helped usher me away from psychological and mental chaos. *A devoted prayer life helped deter me from the temptation to kill.*

On my way home, I pondered my testimony. Jeff's name and forgiveness were both in the same sentence. It hit me: God strategically brought me to California to "pitch my tent at the river Jordan" after my long season of heartbreaks.

So, I thought back to the many invitations that led up to that evening. On January 4, 2016, when I arrived at Sacramento Airport, a lady introduced herself while we were at the baggage claim. She invited me to her church. Bernetta asked me if I had a church during our pedicure and manicure at the nail salon. Maria then invited me to First Baptist Church after reading snippets of her book at the bookstore.

Then, I moved to Southern California and was invited to attend monthly Clergy Coalition (CC) meetings.

At the end of the first CC meeting, I introduced myself to the lady in charge of logistics. I had a name tag on and introduced myself anyway: "Hi, I'm Adrienne."

"Hi, I'm Evelyn," she responded. Then, a black female sheriff's deputy joined in the introduction. I asked for good referrals for beauticians and braiders. The dialogue was so severe, as if I was seeking a cardiologist. What are their credentials? How many of their customers do you know? Do the braiders' customers still have their edges or not? As a black woman, vetting is an intense and serious investment. The conversation ended with a laugh and a sly grin.

"You should attend my church women's luncheon," said Evelyn.

Before I knew it, I started attending Pasadena Church, where Pastor Kerwin and Madelyn Manning are the pastors. I attended the eight o'clock worship service and volunteered at Food for Faith Ministries and twice weekly at the 6 a.m. prayer group. The prayer group was a cross between Shirley Caesar's song, "I Feel Like Praising Him," and Bill Withers's song "Grandma's Hands."

Grandma's hands
Clapped in church on Sunday morning
Grandma's hands
Played a tambourine so well

Grandma's hands
Soothed a local unwed mother
Grandma's hands
Used to lift her face and tell her
She'd say, Baby, grandma understands
That you really love that man
Put yourself in Jesus' hands

If I get to heaven I'll look for
Grandma's hands

I swear, when I entered the church for prayer, it had an aura of sweet frankincense and myrrh. Each member has distinct identities within the body of the church, such as members of the usher board or mother's board, evangelist, choir director, theologian, and Sunday school teacher. I have had the privilege of sitting at the feet of wisdom. Then, I was welcomed to sit at the grown-up table with my sisters, Joyce, Peggy, Annette, Mary, Jeanette, Pat, and Laura. In addition, I attended the 10 a.m. service at Friendship Baptist Church, where Pastor Lucious Smith is the presiding pastor, and the Wednesday night Bible study. That is where I had the spiritual pleasure of meeting Charlene and Al Bailey.

Al said, "I want to invite you to join the small group Bible study we host at our home every Tuesday. You have a zeal for biblical understanding and the Holy Spirit."

I decided to accept the invitation. My first night at the Baileys' was an introduction to a room of spiritual wisdom and a genuine welcoming committee. The Baileys hosted 15 people for a family-style dinner before we dived into the Bible study session and robust discussions. I was intrigued and excited about our view of the biblical text from an African American/black interpretation and perspective. The slave masters were quite selective about the scriptures of the King James Version taught to our enslaved ancestors to reassure them of their servitude. But we can think freely, study the hidden scriptures, and know that Western Civilization had no influence on the text nor told us how to interpret it.

As time passed, I learned that the small group was filled with biblically astute members who had zeal like me. A few times, I experienced deja vu moments as if I was at the Friday night family get-together on the South Side of Chicago—the greeting,

"Hi Adrienne," the philosophical discussions, the soul food dinners, the singing, and the dancing in honor of birthdays and anniversaries. Then, I would return to the present and realize I was with a group of people who had become my SoCal family. I am very grateful to the Baileys' small group: Al and Charlotte Bailey, Alana Bailey Holland, Chanae Hodge, Charles and Evelyn, Alex and LaAja, Dr. D, Ed and Olga, JP, Rashna, Harold, Sally, Sherry, and Lawrence (RIP).

Krista, the William Parnell Center co-director at Fuller Theological Seminary, invited me to the WOC monthly brown bag lunch. This also let me go to other events held on campus. One function that stands out is Martin Luther King's 50th anniversary. I saw Pastor Jean Burk, a member of Fuller's Board of Trustees and board member of the Clergy Coalition. After we spoke, she said, "Are you considering attending the seminary since you frequent campus events?" I said, "Oh no." Then she started to walk away and made an about-face and said, "You don't have any family in California, do you?"

"No Ma'am!"

Then she looked me directly in my eyes and said, "This is a setup. God is setting you up, so you won't have any distractions."

I had no words, just a taken-aback stare. Then I smiled and said thank you.

Richard "Rel" from World Vision Christian humanitarian organization presented at the Clergy Coalition meeting and invited everyone to join the Team World Vision team to prepare for the LA Marathon to raise money for wells on the continent of Africa to help ensure access to clean water for villagers.

Project Fate

Rich was from the suburbs of Chicago, so we had an immediate connection. So, I joined the Pasadena Rose Bowl team. Every Saturday for 12 weeks, we opened the training with prayer thanksgiving and asked for the strength to complete every training session. I chanted, "Thank you, Jesus, thank you Jesus" before, during, and after every run. The Rose Bowl area has hills, curves, and high altitudes.

Lo and behold, God was the wind beneath my wings and the strength behind my back to help me complete my weekly training. The big day was Sunday, March 18, 2018, and I finished the half marathon of 13.1 miles, running 7½ miles and walking the remainder. I'd had four births, three natural and a C-section for my twins, and all were easier than running from LA Dodger Stadium to Hollywood. Dr. Lisa and I partnered and prayed to the Most High amid all the pump-up music playing. Then we looked at each other, from one trainee to another, and took off when that starter pistol was fired. The cheers from the crowd along the routes were uplifting. I was coming down to the wire and the last three miles. Then I saw some brothers dressed in drill team uniforms and forming a drum line. They saw the exhaustion and desperation on my face and were cheering me on, saying, "Come on, sister, you can do it."

I started pointing at the water and Twizzlers while quickly approaching them. One brother extended his long arms and handed me the candy. I gobbled it immediately. I had no more calories and wind. I was delirious because I saw a helicopter in the air with a ladder hanging from it and prayed to God. "Please let them lower the ladder for me. Thank you, Jesus, thank you, Jesus,"

I chanted. Then I saw World Vision's orange flag and Lindsay cheering everyone on by name to the finish line.

I wanted to tell my story of who I was before I became a victim/survivor of domestic violence and a non-offending parent to illustrate how my faith helped sustain me throughout my journey. God was by my side while I was grieving under grace in the Lion's Den.

Epilogue

In May 2018, my former roommate suggested we sign up for a new dating app, Bumble. I replied that I didn't have the bandwidth for another app. She said women can say hello first for safety purposes. I figured I couldn't pass up a safety precaution, so I tried it. One night, we created our profiles with photos and bios and answered some questions. Several days later, a handsome guy and I could chat since a match was formed as we had swiped right on each other's profiles. Well, I took the precautionary steps and greeted James Sar first. He suggested I take the My Personality Quiz and compare our results. That was an exciting suggestion since I haven't taken the Myers & Briggs Personality Test since undergraduate school.

Our personalities were so compatible that we married two years later. On July 10, 2020, the temperature was 112 degrees in Las Vegas. James and I have enjoyed blending our cultures and families. Now, my children have grown to adulthood, and I am proud to see them move through life with grace, resilience, inspiration, and tenacity (GRIT).

During the 2020 pandemic, while I was on medical leave, my former employer released me from my position. I then blended my passion for gender-based violence and reproductive justice into a new career opportunity in the reproductive justice field. Currently, I have created Lapis Analytics Consulting to address the co-occurring challenges of domestic violence and non-offending parents.

Dear Reader

I didn't realize that when God moved me from Illinois to California, that was my Exodus, and I was on the path of deliverance. I don't know what stage of life you're in. But I wish to share that I have had numerous stages, as you have read. I was desperate for God and started chasing after His words and promises. I had to focus on what I knew about myself at every stage, and sometimes I forgot who I was. I had to focus on what I desired for myself and my children and what I believed I could do even in times of distress. I've always thought that God would take me wherever I needed to be because I am the daughter of the Most High. I had to embrace where I came from and who I was. And so I want you to know that whatever stage of life you're in, you can get to wherever you wish to go. You have the capabilities and inspiration to get there. I don't want you to give up on yourself.

I want you to know that God will not give up on you even when it seems unbearable, even if you have scars and a broken heart and don't see God anywhere in sight. I want you to be aware of that. Take each day step by step, bit by bit. You may have to take baby steps or giant steps, but don't stop stepping and know that your story will one day be your testimony. And also, think of it from the perspective of the author Minda Harts, "Who will be the beneficiary of your courage?" So, I encourage you to be who you are, not be afraid, and stand in your truth.

Your divine future is waiting for you.

"I Was So Green I was Blinded By The Truth"

NOTES

Chapter I
Ain't No Party Like a South Side Party

1. (http://www.encyclopedia.chicagohistory.org/pages/1302.html)
2. (https://www.washingtonpost.com/history/2023/11/26/natchez-mississippi-history-slavery)
3. (https://www.history.com/topics/black-history/chicago-race-riot-of-1919)
4. (https://youtube.com/watch?v=PiV4cEOIVKI&feature=shared)
5. (https://www.chicagomag.com/chicago-magazine/august-2016/martin-luther-king-chicago-freedom-movement)

Notes

Chapter III
Invincible Love

6. (https://www.heart.org/en/news/2019/02/20/why-are-black-women-at-such-high-risk-of-dying-from-pregnancy-complications)

Chapter VII
Explosion Phase: Black, Blue, and Broken

7. (https://thegrio.com/2019/04/10/why-some-black-women-refuse-to-call-police-black-male-partners)

8. (www.ifstudies.org) and (www.wianl.org)

Chapter VIII
"A Man Has Always Wanted to Lay Me Down"

9. (https://www.nctsn.org/sites/default/files/resources//domestic_violence_children_qa_domestic_violence_project_advocates.pdf)

10. (https://assets.speakcdn.com/assets/2497/domestic_violence_and_psychological_abuse_ncadv.pdf)

11. (http://saflives.org.uk/psychological-abuse)

12. (https://www.safelivesresearch.org)

13. (https://assets.speakcdn.com/assets/2497/domestic_violence_and_psychological_abuse_ncadv.pdf)

Notes

Chapter IX
The Unbearable Escalation

14. Is it so much to ask Rie Guzman: https://allpoetry.com)

15. "believe in the possibility to heal," (Fariha Ro'isin, https://pen.org/the-pen-ten-fariha-roisin

16. "Restless Ambition," Grace Hartigan, Painter

Chapter X
Turned My Tassel

17. (https://news.wttw.com/2019/11/18/shedding-light-sundown-towns-ropublica-illinois-investigates)

Chapter XI
Inducted into the Non-Offending Parent Club

18. (https://www.nctsn.org/what-is-child-trauma/trauma-types/sexual-abuse)

19. (https://digitalcommons.nl.edu/cgi/viewcontent.cgi?article=1532&context=diss)

20. (https://lundybancroft.com/articles/the-connection-between-batterers-and-child-sexual-abuse-perpetrators)

21. (https://www.vox.com/identities/2018/8/21/17760222/asia-argento-jimmy-bennett-sexual-assault-me-too)

22. (https://lacasacenter.org/why-child-abuse-victims-dont-tell)

23. (htttps://johnprior.attorney/illinois-waves-ggoodbye-statute-limitations-child-sex-abuse/)

24. (http://www.,britannica.com/biography/Delilah)
25. (https://www.nbcnews.com/news/us-news/woman-who-lost-stand-your-ground-case-wants-law-strengthened-n737191)

Chapter XI
D: Means of Escape: Sensual Distraction

26. (https://www.ctpublic.org/arts-and-culture/2018-06-06/a-history-of-racial-disparity-in-american-public-swimming-pools)
27. (https://www.griefstories.org/coping-tools/exploring-art-for-healing)

Chapter XIII
"It's Easier to Build Strong Children Than to Repair Broken Men"

28. (https://www.counseling.org)
29. (https://justiceresearch.dspacedirect.org/items/2fcd629c-d48d-4f7a-96b5-82411b6d6d97)
30. (https://nmaahc.si.edu/explore/stories/recy-taylor-rosa-parks-and-struggle-racial-justice)

www.ingramcontent.com/pod-product-compliance
Lightning Source LLC
Chambersburg PA
CBHW060513090426
42735CB00011B/2204